GARY EUSTICE

PLAYING COPS

And Other Stories That I Tell, Fairly Well

outskirts
press

Playing Cops
and Other Stories that I Tell, Fairly Well
All Rights Reserved.
Copyright © 2020 Gary Eustice
v1.0

The opinions expressed in this manuscript are solely the opinions of the author and do not represent the opinions or thoughts of the publisher. The author has represented and warranted full ownership and/or legal right to publish all the materials in this book.

This book may not be reproduced, transmitted, or stored in whole or in part by any means, including graphic, electronic, or mechanical without the express written consent of the publisher except in the case of brief quotations embodied in critical articles and reviews.

Outskirts Press, Inc.
http://www.outskirtspress.com

ISBN: 978-1-9772-2270-1

Cover Photo © 2020 www.gettyimages.com. All rights reserved - used with permission.

Outskirts Press and the "OP" logo are trademarks belonging to Outskirts Press, Inc.

PRINTED IN THE UNITED STATES OF AMERICA

*I would like to dedicate this book to my lovely
wife Anne, who has accomplished wonders
in civilizing me and keeping me sane.*

Sheriff Donald Eustice

Table of Contents

Preface i
Fields of Glory 1
Driving Lessons 6
Cloudy with a Chance of Death 9
Don't Go Looking for Trouble 15
Troopers vs. Deputies on Highway 52 21
Déjà Vu 39
Gypsy Caravan 43
Hide and Seek 51
Monsters in the Night 55
Dinner and a Show 58
My Mother's Tears 61
People in High Places 65
Porcelain Dolls 68
You Don't Tug on Superman's Cape 71
Runaways 76
Scott 79
Shadow Dancing 83
Shadows 87

The End of Summers 90
The Family Car 101
Rocking Chair Blues 107
Friends Forever 109
Waving the Flag..114
The Old Man in the Corn...118
Big Sticks and Cotton Candy...................................123
Santa and the Sheriff..128
All in the Family 132

Other Stories That I Tell

A Late Summer Samaritan.......................................139
Winter's Discourse..143
Wounded Flower..148
Between Hope and a Hard Place............................154
Christmas Confessions...158
Christmas Eve Messiahs...161
Mental Health Days..165
Dan: The Man with the Plan 172
Dancing with Bears..176
Destiny and Great Love 179
Train of Thought 183
One Cold Winter's Night 186
Snow Rabbit..192
Streams of Life..195
Lessons Learned 198
The Gift..202
We Be In Louisiana 207
Can You Hear Me Now 211

A Christmas Reflection 219
Autumn Blue 222
His Death Not A Whisper Stirred 225
Comin' Down in '73 229
Questions 235

Daydreams, musings, and other delusions
A Little Fiction

The Christmas IOU 245
Another Suck-Ass Day in Paradise 254
Falling for Love 261
Family Transgressions 270
Father and Child Reunion 275
It's a Wonderful Life 283
Red and Purple Hearts 293
Sins of the Father 300
An American Christmas 314
Copasetic 319
When Life Gives You Lemons 329

Preface

IN THE 1960S, one of the most popular TV shows ever, *The Andy Griffith Show,* featured a small-town sheriff who with humor and guile kept his family and friends safe from the evils of the outer world. Sheriff Taylor was fictional; my father was the real deal. During those same years he used his Irish humor and charm to protect his friends and family. Whereas Sheriff Taylor had only one son, Opie, who he worked endlessly to shield from the darker side of life, my father had six sons, and when given the chance to work with him, we were introduced to the vagaries and vicissitudes of life. My brothers and I learned the lessons of a lifetime while still teens. These stories are among the many that we share around the campfire, in remembrance of a time when we were still innocent and found the family work to be a time of joy and sadness, but most rewarding, time spent with our father.

Fields of Glory

I WAS LOOKING forward to my junior year and the football season at St. Johns. I had been moved from fullback to tailback. I would no longer be banging it up the middle in a cloud of dust, but I'd have the chance to use my speed to light fire around the corners. The great plan crashed on the first play of the season. The quarterback called student body right. I had a horde leading me around the right end. Both guards, a tackle, and the fullback were leading me down the field. We swept up the field for twenty yards and I was thinking I was somebody. The pack bunched up and I slowed down with two tacklers around my lower legs. I was standing straight up; I couldn't move or fall down. As I struggled to find some room to topple, I could see another tackler zoning in. I felt panic. I knew it was going to hurt. He hit me square in the left knee and I felt a tear. The pain raced up my leg and hit the brain. It screamed louder than a castrated hog. I fell in tears, not from the injury to the knee, but from an injury to my self-image. I knew it was not going to be the year I had dreamed of.

I continued to play, but it was a struggle. Mid-season we went to Gustavus. My dad was at the game and I really wanted to impress him. Early in the second quarter, I had the chance. Given the ball I ran over the left tackle and I saw the linebacker trip and fall. He was the only obstacle between me and eighty yards of green grass on the way to a touchdown. I took two steps and hurdled over him. In mid-flight I was thinking, *This is fun*. I hit the ground with my left leg, and the knee collapsed again. I was pulled out of the game and spent the rest of the day sitting on the bench.

I was feeling dejected and I was so close to home, I decided to pass up the bus trip back to Collegeville and go home for some good cooking and maybe a little sympathy from my mom. I was riding with my dad through Janesville when he got a call that there had been a murder in Faribault and the suspect had been chased and was hiding in a cornfield near Morristown. All my pain and worries blew by as my dad churned up the gravel roads heading toward the manhunt. I had twenty miles of hard-core adrenaline pumping through my veins when we got to the scene. There were squad cars everywhere. Big men, little men, young men and not so young, all in uniforms of blue or brown, milling around like so many cattle. This is what cops live for, to go beyond the boredom

FIELDS OF GLORY

of their everyday existence and put their mettle to the test.

We drove up and joined the parade of parked squads encircling the unharvested corn. Most of the men had formed into small knots and talked trash, building up their courage. Other men, those with authority, were coordinating with other officers surrounding the corn field, a formal plan. My dad joined the men with the radios. They talked and looked at each other with anxious glances. Finally they were all shaking their heads in accordance. It was going to start. Shotguns appeared and rounds were rapidly being jammed into the firing chambers. Officers took out their sidearms and pulled off the safeties. Everyone was jumpy.

My father motioned for me to meet him at the car. He went to the trunk and took out his riot gun. It was a gleaming oak stock shotgun that had a shortened barrel for a larger spread. I saw everyone pulling out the artillery. This was going to be a serious charge. The plan was to surround the field with officers and then everyone would march forward until contact with the killer was made. It was simple and possibly dangerous.

My dad closed the trunk and loaded his weapon. He then looked at me with surprise. I guess I had become an afterthought. He looked around at all the armed men. I looked around at all the armed men. He stepped into the ditch and kicked around the tall grass. He found a stick. Not a large stick, a stick. He handed me the stick and said, "Get in line."

I took the stick and moved into formation, thinking, *I wish this were a bigger stick*. I swatted a couple of corn stalks and thought, *I really wish this was a much bigger stick. Orchestra conductors have bigger sticks than this.* The men on my side of the field stood about fifty feet apart, waiting for the order to move forward. I knew this kind of tactic worked with deer, but deer weren't armed and didn't shoot first.

Okay, I admit I was scared. I kept thinking, *What if I'm the first to find the chosen one. Should I point my stick at him and ask him to put his gun down, or should I find another stick and offer it to him so that we might have a fair fight?*

The line moved forward. The corn was brown and towered over our heads. I couldn't see the other officers. Sound didn't exist except for the rustling of the corn and the heavy breathing of men on the hunt. Each step my heart beat stronger. Each yard moved me closer to "what?" I wanted to be home. I wanted to be playing football; I wanted to be far, far away. I was pulled with extraordinary strength by the excitement and the fear of the ever tightening trap. I fought to control my body from shaking. I had a great urge to run forward and end the anxiety quickly.

Fifty yards into the field, a radio crackled. Excited voices shouted. The hunted had thrown his gun down and exited on the far side of the field. He was in custody. The ride home took thirty minutes. I was still shaking inside, but I forced calmness to the surface. When I walked into the house, my mom wanted to know how the game went. "Okay," I replied. She then asked my dad how his day had gone. "Okay," he said. "The Johnnies won."

Driving Lessons

I BEGAN DRIVING in the summer of 1967. I was sixteen. My father had a special system for teaching his boys the dangers of driving. He believed in the "scared straight" approach to driver's education.

My first lesson occurred on a sweltering August afternoon. I was in the yard when my father burst from the house in an agitated frenzy that only life and death ignited. He yelled on the run for me to join him.

As the family station wagon rocketed down the driveway, the radio was bursting with frantic instructions. We were racing to a deadly traffic accident with multiple reported deaths. At these times the family station wagon transformed itself into a squad car when my father hit the siren and put the magnetic red light on the roof. As needed the car also served as ambulance or hearse.

As we raced to the accident site, my father drove by instinct. His car hugged each turn and corner with years of familiarity. Intersections were ninety-degree sliding turns. Wheels would lock as we entered the turn and then he'd push the accelerator to launch us down the straightaway. The siren wailed out a warning to unsuspecting cows and people alike.

We arrived at a remote country intersection; it was guarded on all sides by swaying seas of corn. Two cars were at rest in opposite ditches. Two bodies lay on the road. Shattered glass and crumpled steel locked other victims inside metal tombs.

Running toward the survivors, we were joined by the owner of the Waseca Mobil Gas station. He owned the only real ambulance in the county. We triaged the injured. There was no time for the nausea to take hold.

The most seriously injured were placed in the ambulance. The less injured were carried to the family station wagon. The backseat was laid down and the injured were placed in the back. Sirens parted the growing crowds, and the ambulance and family car began the hurried mission of delivering the injured to the hospital.

I assisted in carrying the dead to the side of the road and covered them with sheets. Then we turned our attention to the uninjured. That's when I first noticed Michael. He was a beautiful boy. He was maybe two years old. He had hair the color of spring corn tassel and eyes the color of the summer sky. My father laid him in my arms. He looked so small and fragile. I cradled him and carried him into the shade of a parked car. I rested my back against the car door and slid down into the graveled road shoulder.

Michael looked straight ahead, dazed by all the frantic activity. He never complained. I gently rocked him in the unforgiving heat. I hummed the lullabies my mother had sung to me. I gingerly tousled his hair and blew away offending insects that attempted to alight on his face.

In the serenity of the moment, the clouds in the great blue sky appeared as giant sails on passing ships. The corn swayed in the wind and its gentle to-and-fro motion put me into a trance. I rocked Michael to the magic of the dancing corn. Michael, a good, good boy, just stared ahead and appeared so very, very tired.

When the ambulance returned, I placed Michael quietly on a stretcher. I ran my hand through his hair and, smiling, promised him everything would be fine.

My dad went to the hospital to check on everyone, and I caught a ride home. I was shooting baskets when my father's car rolled into the driveway. He got out of the car obviously overcome with the pain and trauma of the day. "How's the little guy?" I called out.

My dad stopped in his tracks and with his back turned to me replied, "He died."

I was holding the basketball with both hands. It slipped from my grip and started to bounce down the driveway on a solo journey to nowhere.

Cloudy with a Chance of Death

ON THE EVENING of Sunday, April 30, 1967, my brothers and I were sitting on the roof of our home watching the black boiling clouds from the south approach Waseca. It was more entertaining than Ed Sullivan. We'd wrestle and jostle for position. "Hey, look at those clouds!" someone would yell, and we'd all stop and watch in wonder. The sky was an angry sea with great black waves rolling in. Fearsome clouds, one after another, tumbling on top of each other. The storm passed and all became freakishly quiet. The stillness pulled the air from the lungs. Then the siren on city hall began to wail. Its cry alerted Waseca to a fact some residents already knew. A tornado had ascended and destroyed the southeastern corner of the community.

My parents had been visiting in a neighboring community. When they had learned of the storm's approach they immediately started home. As they traveled the skies turned angry and my father pushed hard on the gas pedal, and when he heard radio chatter of a possible tornado touchdown, he hit the siren. The last five miles to town were covered in an instant. He dropped my mother at the bottom of the driveway. Doug and I had climbed down from the roof and were standing in the yard. He yelled for us to join him and we sped through town to the scene of the storm's great destruction. We paid no attention to the stop signs or the awkward skyward gazes of citizens just beginning to learn of the death and destruction that had dropped down from heaven upon their neighbors. As we raced to the death scene, it was now a beautiful spring evening with birds singing sweetly.

We approached the storm-ravaged section of town, and debris began to appear here and there. Small branches became large limbs; soon whole trees lay across streets and yards. Appliances, furniture, and unmatched pieces of buildings and homes were differentially scattered everywhere. We came upon the apocalypse. People stood dazed where homes had been wrenched from their foundations. Other people were scrambling through debris calling the names of those unaccounted for. We had to walk several blocks to get into the center of the madness. If the community had been made of toy blocks, then it appeared as though a large and angry child had just spilled over his box of toys and stomped them into nothingness.

CLOUDY WITH A CHANCE OF DEATH

God had had his tantrum.

The police, sheriff's deputies, volunteer firemen, and good Samaritans began appearing from all corners of the community. I followed my dad into the melee. He was in his element. He was in command. A man stood outside a house that had completely fallen in on itself. He spoke softly to himself. "I think there are people in there." My father called to several men to help. Doug and I picked up the top of a toppled wall. We were joined by others and we gave a great heave and began to stand the wall back up. We had it nearly erect when we all noticed in unison a body. It may have been my imagination, but it appeared flattened by the wall. It certainly was small for a grown man. My mind was twisting like a tornado with competing thoughts circling and fighting each other to make sense of what lay before me. Death so raw is unnerving. It turns the mind cold and slows down reactions. I felt as if I had been hit by a large piece of debris. I couldn't make sense of the crumpled man who lay so silently next to his dinner plate.

We searched several more homes before the massiveness of the task hit. My father asked me to call members of the high school wrestling team and get as much help as we could muster and meet at the sheriff's office in half an hour. I ran to the car and headed home to use the phone. As I pulled away, my dad was climbing into the seat of a city patrol car and heading to the office. We were both running to find help and some hope. I felt connected to my dad like I had never felt before. We were on the same mission and he was counting on me.

I made calls and met the Romes and Edwards at the sheriff's office in twenty minutes. My dad was on the phone furiously delivering orders and instructions. Between commands on the phone, he had us raise our right hands and he swore us in as official deputies of Waseca County. It was the first and only time he ever officially swore me in for duty. The usual practice was to just show up and get busy. We put our hands down and sprinted to our cars. We were now on duty. Testosterone-driven teen brother combinations bent on rushing into the unknown. I looked back to see my dad as determined as I had ever seen him returning to his car and speeding off to the fractured neighborhood.

That would be the last time I would see him for three days. He would not sleep or change clothes for the next seventy-two hours as he took control of the devastated community and worked to turn back the crimes of nature.

When the wrestling team arrived, the search had become more focused and deliberate. A hasty count had been made to determine who and how many people were still unaccounted for. An elderly woman was missing. Someone suggested she may have been blown into the lake. I knew of a pontoon we could commandeer. A fireman gave me a pair of large grappling hooks, and the Romes, the Edwards, and I went to Thompsons Boat House and pirated the largest pontoon boat anchored at the dock. We set course for the southern bay of Clear Lake, tying large heavy-duty ropes to the grappling hooks and talking excitedly about the large fish we were about to catch.

Teen boys trying to hide their nervousness become macho assholes. We didn't want to talk about death or dead people, so we talked in code about large blue fish and who would be the first to land one. We lined the pontoon up between Thompsons Boat House and Maplewood Park, threw the great hooks out, and began slowly passing back and forth across the southern half of the lake. Boards and pieces of wall floated past and bumped against us. The lake was a stew of broken homes and lost dreams.

We immediately began to snag unseen things in the water. Excitedly we'd yell out, "I've got something," hoping to be the one to find the body, but afraid at the same time of being the one who found the body. Heroes are often fearful folk doing what's right, all the while stuffing the panic in their stomachs and hoping not to choke on the fear should it rise to the throat.

It was getting dark and we were discussing stopping the search till morning when Doug Edwards yelled, "I've something big." The rope was pulled taut. Doug was pulling on something at the back of the boat. We all grabbed on and joined in the tug of war with the dark waters. Someone cut the engine and we all pulled feverishly. This could be it. When the body broke to the service, anxiety bound us together. Someone yelled something about a whale and we all began juvenile chatter about landing the biggest fish of our lives. It was the fear of touching death that had us talking like idiots. As the body came toward the boat, we became reverent. Silence replaced the inane talk, and compassion became the glue that now held the team together. She was a large woman and the water made her slippery. Doug and I jumped into the water and pushed as the others pulled gently. It may have been the first time that some of the guys had ever seen death. It was a quiet ride back to the mooring. The night ended our adventures and we all went home and slept fitfully. Tugging on death's shroud is not an adventure or a thing to speak of in public. It is humbling.

Don't Go Looking for Trouble

IN THE LATE 1960s, singer/songwriter Charlie Maguire was singing, "Don't go looking for trouble; trouble will find you anyway." I loved the song, knew all the words, hadn't contemplated the prophecy it contained.

Late August of 1968 meant the football season was beginning and the Teen Canteen would be in full swing on Saturday evenings. The Sheriff's Department sponsored teen dances at the 4-H building on the fairgrounds in Waseca. The best state and regional bands ripped it up. Occasionally even national top-charting groups made appearances. I never missed the dances.

That Saturday was warm. Dog days of August in Minnesota meant that the dogs stayed in the shade panting, and all who ventured out dripped from the heat and humidity. The dogs were barking and it was hot! The evening would be cool though, and the coolest place to be would be the fairgrounds and the big dance. I was dressed and ready to go an hour early. I was calling around to find out who was and was not going to make an appearance. My dad got a late call and had to head down to the office. He pulled me aside and asked if I could help out the deputies chaperoning the dance as they would be short staffed. "No problem," I said.

"Stay out of trouble," he said.

"Always." I chuckled.

The dances had two primary rules. No one was admitted who had been drinking, and no one over twenty-one was allowed in. With deputies walking around, the dancers were always well-behaved, and trouble stayed far away.

The Underbeats were pounding out a hard rhythm and I was lost in a trance spinning and stomping around the dance floor. The song ended and everyone was cheering and clapping. Teen exuberance reigned. The band announced a break and I headed outside to get some air.

As I passed by the ticket booth at the entrance, an argument was heating up. Two obviously older bikers had tried to get in. The deputies had rightly stopped them and were instructing them that they were not allowed as the dance was for younger people only. Dressed in their leathers and bandannas, the bikers were attempting to intimidate the older deputies. Mert, the county's chief deputy, was holding his cool. He blocked the bikers and pushed them outside. Mert

DON'T GO LOOKING FOR TROUBLE

went back behind the counter and noticed me coming through. "Gary, keep an eye on them," and nodded his head toward the door.

I walked outside and sat on the hood of a squad car parked just outside the entrance. Dozens of kids were milling about in small groups excitedly gesturing and talking. Two bikers stood among the dancers and were drunkenly complaining of their poor treatment. Another half-dozen bikers stayed with their bikes at the back of the parking lot. The two drunken bikers were getting louder and more demonstrative. As their voices rose, so did my teen exuberance.

I remained sitting on the car hood watching and waiting for whatever would come next. They were Mutt and Jeff. The quieter one was large, six foot, well over 250 pounds. The smaller man was less than five-foot-eight, but he had a mean and chiseled look. The small man was the loudest. The big guy seemed to be trying to calm him down. I just watched, maybe too hard, too intensely. The little guy caught my gaze and yelled, "What the hell you looking at?"

Now, can anyone answer me, why is it always the little guys?

He came my way. I tried to appear relaxed, but my sphincter muscle was tightening. He got in my face and I noticed drool on the sides of his mouth. His eyes were dilated and dark. His reddened face screamed anger.

"What are you looking at?"

I looked down. I didn't want this challenge.

"What's your problem, asshole?"

"Nothing," I squeaked. I should have stopped there, but sometimes I would engage my mouth without thinking. "You were told you couldn't get in if you had been drinking."

"Who's been drinking?"

Now I was trying to tiptoe out of a problem. "You look like you've been drinking."

"Who's been drinking?"

I started to look around, my arms and legs trembling. My voice was cracking. My back was to the windshield of the car. I was trapped on the hood. There was a telephone pole to my right. A crowd was gathering to my left cutting me off. Trouble had found me. I squeaked, "You smell like you've been drinking."

Now I'd never been in a fight in my life, outside of my brothers. I was scared. My mind was doing cartwheels trying to get me out of this jam. I couldn't run. I didn't want to cry, but I was going to. I wanted to submit, but how do you do that when this guy obviously wanted my ass on a platter, and I was surrounded by screaming and chanting peers. I was trapped and there was only one answer. The correct answer. The God-given truth. I braced myself for what was coming next as I opened my mouth and very timidly said, "You've been drinking."

I knew I was in trouble. I saw it coming and couldn't stop it. His fist seemed to come from yards behind his head, and I watched it in slow motion launch at my face. It hit my jaw. I erupted with adrenaline and reaction. I jumped off the car. I yelled to Mert, "We've got one." I grabbed the dude by his jacket and threw him into the telephone pole. I saw his back wrap around the pole like a rubber band and spring back toward me. He bounced off the pole onto the car hood. I had my hands in his mouth as if I was trying to pull his lower jaw off his face while at the same time I was pounding his head into the hood. It was as if I was watching myself and I was thinking, *Are you crazy? Look at what you're doing.* I frightened myself, but I was in the moment and kept pounding his head into the car. Then I thought, *Shit, the big guy is behind me.* I threw the little guy off the car into the crowd and turned to face a much bigger danger. Just as I turned I saw a large oak stick strike the large biker across his back, knocking him to the ground. Mert stood over him coiled, ready to strike again.

The bikers were quickly handcuffed and placed in the squad car. They were bitter men. As the car pulled away to take them to jail, I walked up to the squad car and knocked on the window next to where the little guy sat. "You don't mess with the sheriff's kid!" I yelled. He spit on the window.

My friends were all over me, slapping me on the back and telling me how crazy it all was and, man, how I had shown those guys. I was shaking all over. I couldn't stop the trembling. I was frightened by my behavior. I couldn't grasp where the rage had come from. I scared myself.

The band started up again and everyone went inside. I was still scared. I had to do something with the surging energy and anxiety. I ran home. I snuck into the house and went straight to my room. Falling on my bed, I cried. I was so confused and scared by my violence.

It took me hours to calm down. It took several days for me to admit that it had all been my fault. I didn't need to go looking for trouble. It found me anyway.

Troopers vs. Deputies on Highway 52

HERE'S THE SHORT of it. I'm standing spread-eagled on the back of a highway trooper's car. He's got his gun drawn pointing at my back. My buddy Scoop has assumed the position next to me. The cop is nervous; he thinks we're kidnappers. He believes we're dangerous and he's not taking any chances. My dad is in street clothes trying to tell the cop that he's the sheriff and we're his deputies. My younger brother Todd is yelling at the cop, "I'm with them!" I'm thinking, *Wow, this could make a good story*. So, here's the long of it.

There are eighty-seven counties in the state of Minnesota. It was said that Minnesota had eighty-six county sheriffs and one sheriff-at-large. That was my dad, or Deputy Don as my friends called him. He didn't believe in county boundaries or judicial jurisdictions. If a wrong needed righting and no one else had the common sense to make the correction, he had to see it done. He had an absolute abiding faith in the rule of fairness, and at times that faith slammed up against the rule of law. At those times "doing right" was more important than doing the legal thing. So, it wasn't uncommon that he would go about settling unjust conditions by ignoring the law and just doing the "right thing." This was one of those situations.

Let's back up two months—that's when the great plan unfolded. I sat at my parents' kitchen table with my parents and the Lofgrens. The Lofgrens were old friends of the family. Dolores had grown up with my mother in Waseca. She had come to ask for my father's help. Her oldest daughter, Nancy, had been seduced into a cult. They had not heard from her for more than two years. In the early months of her conversion she had sent angry letters scolding her parents for being a part of all the world's wrongs and castigating them for their sinful ways. Then the letters stopped. The Lofgrens had heard many frightening stories of this cult and its leader. The Great Rama had mixed equal amounts Christianity and Hinduism with a sprinkling of good old American entrepreneurism and devised a religion that promised all true believers would drive to heaven in the End Days in their very own Cadillacs. I assume Elvis would have approved.

The Lofgrens had approached lawyers, judges, and other associated legal contortionists. Doors were quietly, politely, and quickly closed. Nothing could be done. The Lofgrens could not accept that their daughter could be held hostage and they refused to face the frightening future possibility of life without their daughter. So they came to my father seeking solace and hoping for a miracle, man-made of course.

This was the plan. The "church group" met on Sunday mornings at a motel in Rochester. The Lofgrens would get details of the times the membership met and when Nancy might be in attendance. They had a mole on the inside. My job was to recruit other "deputies" for the pickup. Sounded like great fun. Snatch and run. That is exactly how deeply any of us thought it through. Other than to say there were rumors that the sheriff and county attorney in Rochester had been informed of the plan and had agreed that if a call should come into the law enforcement center in Olmsted County, it would be politely put aside and forgotten.

I heard nothing for weeks. I had recruited Scoop to deputy up with me. He was fresh out of the military and professed to now be an expert in Tai Kwando. He was a high school buddy and he had covered my back on other occasions, like a time in New Ulm. A gang of kids in New Ulm had been attacking athletic teams for laughs and chuckles during my senior year in high school. They had attacked the Waseca basketball team. When the wrestling team traveled to New Ulm a couple of weeks later, we had been warned by the coaches not to look for trouble. After

PLAYING COPS

the wrestling meet the team was eating in a restaurant downtown. One of the lightweights, who had left the meal and gone to the team bus, came back and told Scoop and me that a teammate was surrounded by a gang of brawlers right next to the bus. Scoop and I got up, and not wanting to look for trouble, we didn't tell the coaches where we were going. When we got to the bus, the teammate was corralled and someone had knocked his glasses off. The specs lay at his feet and he was being taunted to pick them up. He was cautious enough not to. He would have been sucker-punched. I looked for Scoop to assist in formulating a plan. Scoop had already waded into the crowd and placed himself between the angry punks and our teammate. I pushed my way in to stand next to Scoop. I didn't know about Scoop, but I had thought we were going to negotiate. We pushed the gang back so our friend could get his glasses, and then Scoop just started swinging. We were in the middle of it when the bus driver came running and the New Ulm kids ran. So you can see why I picked Scoop. He didn't need a plan; you just had to point him in the direction you wanted to go and he got you there.

I was living on a farm outside of Waseca with friends. We had developed a spring ritual of catching a couple garbage cans full of Lake Superior smelt and inviting anyone who liked beer out to the farm for a smelt fry and assorted refreshments. We even had a theme. We called it the Ed Geen Memorial Ball. Ed was a serial killer and cannibal from Wisconsin. We felt he was just misunderstood, so the Ball's theme was "Have a Heart, Support Ed Geen." On this particular last day of April, Scoop could not attend the spring soiree, as he had to be in a wedding. Halfway through the night I got a call that the freeing of the religious captive, Nancy Lofgren, was on. My younger brother Todd called and asked if he could be part of the rescue mission. Why not include him. He was available. The next day was a Sunday and he usually couldn't find his shoes to go to church. I believe that his lost shoes had more to do with the *Three Stooges* and professional wrestling being telecast on Sunday mornings than that Todd actually lacked any spiritual guidance in his life. I was able to locate Scoop and suggested he stop drinking as I would pick him up at 6 a.m. on the next day, May 1st. That gave both of us four hours to sober up.

I was up at 5:30 and I gingerly stepped over the reclining bodies of partygoers who had not quite left the property yet. I wanted to look nondescript, so I had on jeans and a leather bomber jacket. I smelled my T-shirt; the beer on it had not gone stale yet. I picked up my brother and we swung by Scoop's. He came out wearing a light blue tux that he had obviously slept in. He had no shirt or socks, just the tux. I mentioned the lack of socks. Scoop explained that his brand of martial arts included kicks and he would simply shed his shoes and become a lethal weapon.

PLAYING COPS

The sun was just breaking when we headed into the east. We were driving my Firebird. I had fallen for this car because a popular TV detective, Rockford, drove one just like it. We discussed a plan. I had been a high school sprinter, so I'd do the snatch. Scoop would stay at the car and get my back. As my car was a two-door, Todd would make sure the doors were open and the seats folded forward, for an easy deposit. Satisfied we had covered all the bases, we sat back for the hour's drive. It started to snow. May 1st and it was snowing. We laughed, joking that the fluffy stuff might be a bad omen.

We arrived in Rochester and checked out the hotel, which sat on the intersection of two four-lane highways, with a large parking lot and not many customers. Scoop and I entered to survey the church area, just in case it had to go down inside. We used the public men's room as the beer was still making its way out of our bodies. One of the toilets decided to overflow. We tiptoed out, laughing that nothing else could possibly go wrong.

My parents had arrived with the Lofgrens. My youngest siblings were with them, Barry and Barb, both under ten. We all went to a nearby restaurant so the kids could eat and the adults could watch. Lloyd Lofgren offered to sit with us in the parking lot. We concurred. I hadn't seen Nancy in ten years, and she had reportedly lost an enormous amount of weight. There were stoplights at the first intersection we'd have

TROOPERS VS. DEPUTIES ON HIGHWAY 52

to travel through. My dad would block them with his car. With plans finalized my parents ordered breakfast for the family, and Lloyd joined Scoop, Todd, and me back in the parking lot.

We again positioned ourselves in the back of the parking lot. I was in the driver's seat, Scoop rode shotgun, and Todd and Lloyd were sitting in the back. We settled in for a long wait, and began to chat talk. We did congratulate ourselves on our choice of parking space as we could see everything and anything in the lot. Lloyd was sharing how much he missed his daughter when a large passenger van came into the lot and parked right next to us. Then a second van and a third van parked and people began getting out and walking toward the motel. Lloyd was shaking and excitedly whispered, "That's her."

Back in the restaurant my dad turned to Barry and said, "Watch this. This will be interesting."

I asked Lloyd for a quick description. He pointed toward one girl. She was a hundred feet from the car when I fully understood which girl he was pointing at. Scoop and I got out. Scoop came around to the driver's side and stood next to me, shoeless. I quickly walked toward the group of thirty or more. When I got close I called, "Nancy!" and a young woman turned. I dashed to her and scooped her up, threw her over my shoulder, and sprinted for the car. Scoop had assumed a defensive position. He stood at a ninety-degree angle, legs spread for balance and his arms up in classic karate form, and he was yelling at my pursuers to stay back, "This is police business." The adrenaline was pumping and I didn't recognize the surreal nature of the scene unfolding. A group of devout believers had just had a member of their congregation snatched up by a young man in jeans and a leather jacket and most likely reeking of beer, and we were all stampeding in the direction of another man standing shirtless and shoeless in a soiled tux, demanding my pursuers stop as we were working for the police.

Nancy was screaming, as any true crime victim should. Todd had the car seat down and I laid Nancy into the backseat with her father. Todd ran around to the passenger side and got in and Scoop and I followed. We locked the doors just as the frenzied mob reached the car and started pulling on the doors and rocking the car. A man later identified as the cult's local minister threw himself spread-eagle across the hood of the car. He was screaming but I was deaf from the excitement. I started the car and threw it into first gear and we lurched out of the crowd and I picked up speed as we torched the ditch. I hit the pavement and the minister flew skyward. An act of God?

As I came out of the ditch, my father came from nowhere with his siren blazing and blocked the oncoming traffic. Two minutes ago he was having breakfast with his family; now they were all in his car, eyes saucer size, staring down traffic as it all came to a screeching halt. I shot by my dad's blockade, my car

TROOPERS VS. DEPUTIES ON HIGHWAY 52

fishtailing as if waving goodbye. We were traveling fast, but nothing compared to the rapid pounding of our hearts. I flew off Highway 14 and pointed the car north on 52 heading to Minneapolis. We were in the clear. Mission accomplished. The buzzing in my head dissipated, I lost my cold, steel focus, and I sat back. I looked at Scoop. He had a shit-eating grin that didn't stop. I nodded to him. "Everyone okay?" Quickly everyone replied, "Yes." Surprisingly even Nancy. I hadn't noticed the screaming had stopped. Somewhere between our flight out of the ditch and doing a ninety-degree turn at eighty miles an hour, Nancy had recognized her father. "Oh, it's you." They then had settled into catching up on family. Nancy was excited, telling her father how much she loved and missed all of the family. Scoop started reading the Sunday paper, beginning with the funnies and moving on to the sports section. I put on the cruise control and sat back anticipating smooth sailing.

Ten miles into our journey, my father caught up and signaled for us to pull over. He pulled in behind us. Mrs. Lofgren had followed in her car and she joined the chain of vehicles on the roadside. My dad asked how we were all doing. Mrs. Lofgren leaned in and kissed Nancy and they shared a huge hug. My dad decided all was well and he said goodbye and turned around to take his family home. Todd got into the Lofgrens' vehicle with Mrs. Lofgren. They were going to follow me into the cities. Everyone congratulated everyone. Final hugs and kisses were shared and once again we hit the highway.

I felt smug that we had accomplished a good thing. Father and daughter were having quite a reunion and Scoop was back at the paper. I turned on the radio and was singing along with the Eagles to "Tequila Sunrise" when I noticed Scoop lower the paper and in a very low and serious voice say, "Oh, shit, look at that."

I looked directly out my side window. Keeping pace with me was a maroon Minnesota Highway Patrol car. The officer had his gun drawn and pointed at me. He was mouthing big slow words. I concentrated on his lips. "Pull over now!" He emphasized his words with the exclamation point of his drawn gun.

I pulled over immediately. I knew this was a mistake. He did not understand. I threw open the car and jumped out to try to offer an explanation to the officer. He was already on the pavement, with his gun drawn and pointed directly at me, somewhere in center mass, or in civilian speech, at my heart. "Stop or I'll shoot."

I kept moving forward. "You don't understand…"

"Stop right there!"

"Let me explain."

"I said stop!"

Somewhere deep in the recesses of my brain, something screamed. I got the message. I froze. His gun remained pointed at my heart. Nancy started

TROOPERS VS. DEPUTIES ON HIGHWAY 52

screaming as if on cue. "Help me, help me, I've been kidnapped."

I put my hands up and moved to the trunk of my car and lay across it as ordered. Scoop soon joined me. The officer yelled to Mr. Lofgren to identify himself. He said he was Nancy's father. Nancy concurred but kept screaming she been kidnapped.

My brother Todd and Mrs. Lofgren had caught up to us, and Todd came running up to the scene to offer assistance. He kept talking to the officer, insisting, "I'm with them," pointing to Scoop and myself. A car of old ladies pulled over; two jumped out and started taking pictures. I was shaking in fear. *I've become a tourist attraction*.

My dad had been driving home when he saw the northbound trooper. Hoping there wasn't any trouble, he turned around just to make sure. He came upon the chaotic scene and approached the trooper in his civilian clothes. He was trying to tell the trooper this was all a big mistake. The trooper didn't know him, and my father didn't have his badge. Everyone was talking at once. Two other squad cars came wailing in. All officers exited their squads with guns drawn. I prayed Scoop and I weren't going to be target practice. Unsure of what was going on, the trooper acted professionally. He cuffed Scoop and me and placed us in a squad. We all headed back to the sheriff's office in Rochester to try to straighten it all out. At that point I wasn't so sure I had an explanation.

PLAYING COPS

If there was to have been collusion, it never happened. The Olmsted County sheriff never made it into the office that morning, so when the teletype sent out an all-points bulletin, it was taken very seriously except in Waseca, where Deputy Neidt read the teletype, including my car's license number. He ran the number and when it came back in my name, he simply said aloud to himself, "What's Don up to now?"

Scoop and I were escorted to a cell while things were being "straightened out." We could hear things being discussed. Scoop was to be married in a few weeks and he began bemoaning how he would not be able to explain his absence at the ceremony to his wife. "She can read, can't she?" I quipped. "You're going to be famous. Who do you want to be, Bonnie or Clyde?" Scoop wasn't into the levity of the moment.

While Scoop and I sat in the cooler, Nancy and her parents had been placed in a room alone, near the back door to the jail and close to their car. My mom and my siblings were hanging around the outer office with the true believers. The brethren were on the floor, heads down, praying for Nancy's safe return. They chanted in unison, sometimes punctuated by a chorus of wails.

We heard the earnestness of the conversation between law enforcement officials turn to laughter. My dad must have won the major points of the discussion, but it had taken two hours. Two long hours. Scoop and I were relieved when they came to let us out and we joined my parents. None of the Lofgrens were around. Apparently Nancy had consented to travel with her parents to the cities. No one had mentioned it to her congregation; they remained glued to the floor, continuing their nonstop vigil. Scoop and I decided to flee the scene. My mom asked us to stop by the Waseca County jail and check on the dinner cooking for the prisoners. We waded through the prostrate prayer party and started home, nervously laughing about the morning but secretly knowing we had some good stories to tell.

That evening phone calls began coming into my parents' home. Threatening calls. Death threats. "Watch your kids. We know where you live." An unknown car sat at the end of the driveway. In their haste to keep my parents under surveillance, they had not driven around the block, but instead just pulled up in front of the house. We had two driveway entrances. Todd and I walked down the back and circled around to the front. We jumped on the bumper and pounded on the hood. They sped away that night. They returned later and kept up a harassment of surveillance for weeks.

For the next few weeks, Scoop and I regaled all with our adventures into cop land. Nancy was at a private home being deprogrammed, and word was she was doing well. She was conversing regularly with her parents and asking about other family members. All seemed right with the world. But then…

PLAYING COPS

I was visiting my parents when the phone rang. It was business as my dad had that professional tone. Then his voice softened and he turned white. "What are you saying?" I had never seen him so nervous. "Nancy ran? Where would she run to?"

Nancy had been allowed to take a walk by herself as a reward for doing so well. She went to the first phone booth and called her church leaders. They swept her up and she was back at the cult. She was making anew the accusations that she had been kidnapped. All that had been settled unraveled. The FBI wanted to talk to us!

I knew we were in real trouble when my dad said we'd be meeting with an attorney before speaking with the FBI. The Scoop was unsettled. I couldn't blame him. I'd been around this cop stuff all my life and I knew we had a lot of explaining to do, and it all better be good and coordinated.

We met with John McLoone the IV. He was a local attorney, intelligent, an Irish pit bull. My dad had the greatest respect for John. He was brilliant and he had the gift of blarney. He actually had swayed jurors and judges with the honey of his sweet arguments. We met several times and went over our stories, or testimony, to make sure details matched. We had picked up Nancy with the intention of taking her to a psychiatric hospital in Minneapolis. My dad had filled out the pickup order. We had all been acting within the framework of the law.

TROOPERS VS. DEPUTIES ON HIGHWAY 52

I don't remember much about my meeting with the Feds. I walked to the sheriff's office, where the questioning was to be done. Outside the building were two men smoking. They were lean and had on matching black suits with white shirts. Pretty typical. I recalled that I had wanted to join the FBI when I had graduated from college. I even went so far as to get an application. It included a health review form that had height and weight charts. At six feet I could not weigh more than 165 pounds to be an agent. I hadn't weighed that since the sixth grade. I would have had to become anorexic to be a G-man. I couldn't imagine myself looking like Twiggy and wearing black.

People with power impressed and scared me. I'm sure I was very nervous talking to the FBI. I probably avoided eye contact and was very polite. I'm sure I squirmed a little. They were very businesslike. They took lots of notes and never betrayed their personal thoughts. I doubt I was with them for more than half an hour. When questioning was completed I do remember a great sense of relief that I was actually walking out of the jail.

Feds poking around wasn't enough. Now a grand jury investigation was being launched. The county prosecutor from Olmsted—rumors had put him in knowledge of our little foray before it happened—now was shaking sabers and demanding that all facts come forward. All facts except any knowledge of duplicity and/or conspiracy.

There were many meetings with attorneys. On the opening day of the investigation, we were all summoned back to Rochester. We again waded through the sea of devoted derrieres pointed skyward in hope that those new Cadillacs would soon appear. They chanted and prayed in unison. We walked through and around them. It was like walking through a flower garden and being very careful not to step on a delicate petal.

Again my memory fails me. I remember the feelings, however: fear, anxiety, and a great wish to run away. The prosecutor hammered at me. I was mentally exhausted leaving the stand. Scoop went on the stand later in the day. The prosecutor led him through his testimony, looking for stray details that wouldn't match my version of the day. He bullied and cajoled Scoop. Scoop met him head-on and never varied from the well-practiced story. Near the end of Scoop's testimony, the prosecutor came to the place where Scoop and I had been released and we were getting instructions from my parents on what to do as we left the Olmsted County Jail. The prosecutor was hoping to connect us to Nancy's second disappearance as now that, too, was a part of the greater conspiracy.

"So you were released from jail and standing on the steps. Did you know at that time that Nancy's parents had taken her out the back door and were in the process of transporting her to be deprogrammed?"

"No I did not, sir."

"Did you speak to anyone at that time?"

"Yes, I talked to Don Eustice and his wife."

"By Don Eustice, do you mean your codefendant Sheriff Eustice?"

"Yes."

"Did Sheriff Eustice give you any instructions before you left the jail that day?"

"No, he didn't, but Mrs. Eustice took us aside and spoke to us."

The attorney leaned in, sensing a kill. "What did Mrs. Eustice say to you. What were her instructions?" Turning back he smiled to the jury to emphasize the importance of this last question.

Scoop was rattled by the attorney's sneer, but he stayed on task; he looked straight at the jury and confidently spoke. "She asked Gary and I to stop by the jail in Waseca and to turn down the heat on the roast."

What proceeded became the longest grand jury deliberation in the history of the state, before a decision not to charge us criminally was made. Relief is a small word for the extreme stress lifted from our lives.

***

Postscript

In the fall of 2008, Nancy left the cult on her own free will after many years of abuse. She described a life lived under extreme control. She wasn't allowed to wear glasses. She lost tremendous weight due to a diet poor in nutrition, particularly protein. Protein powers thought, and thoughts were forbidden. She had been forced to marry a man she barely knew. She saw men, women, and children abused. She left two children and several grandchildren behind.

She found a safe house and a job in northern Wisconsin. I heard that she was working at a fast-food restaurant. I paid her a visit. I entered the business and saw her taking orders from a family. I approached her from behind and called her name.

"Nancy."

She turned.

Smiling and offering my hand, I said, "Hi. The last time we met, I swept you off your feet."

"Oh, you're one of them," and she finished taking the order.

Déjà Vu

I FOLLOWED THE sheriff's car into the farmyard. Starlight shimmered and danced on the ground and added shadows to the huge drifts that lined the driveway. I stepped out of my car and the snow crunched like cereal. I tapped my left foot in a small arch and enjoyed the sound of the snow's destruction. A deputy called out to me and I snapped back to the seriousness of the situation. "I thought I saw someone run into the barn. Go into the house and stay warm. We'll check out the barn and the outbuildings." The deputy and his partner started toward the darkness. I looked at the old wood-frame farmhouse and smiled at the sight of smoke curling out of its chimney and decided to heed their advice.

I hoped for a quick end to this endeavor. I had given up a late dinner with my wife for this. My father had been a rural sheriff, and I hated the fact that he had been gone so often. All my life, the family had taken second place to my father's job. I had promised myself I would never let work become that important. So here I was trudging through knee-deep snow, and my family was sitting around a cold dinner waiting for me to return.

Earlier that evening my stomach had jumped when the phone rang. No one called me in the evening unless it was work related. Less than a week had passed since the last unpleasant round of pleas and threats from my wife regarding my devotion to work taking precedence over my family. She was correct. I was too involved in my work. I told myself it was necessary, but I had choices.

I excused my behavior because the sheriff was the chairman of the board, and oversaw the operations of the small community mental health center that employed me. The sheriff believed that violence was a sign of mental illness. Following that bit of reasoning, it only made sense to have a therapist available whenever there was a threat of violence. That and the fact that I was twice the size of most of his deputies made it quite convenient to have me on the scene.

I followed a narrow, worn path through the snow to the house. I promised myself this would be the last time I left my family for work. That's what killed my father. He had to make one more house call when he should have said no to work and gone home and been with his family. He walked into his death, when he should have been with his family on a weekend

DÉJÀ VU

outing. Only he couldn't say no to his job, so instead of enjoying the state fair, he made one more call and walked into one more potentially dangerous situation. His last walk was toward a small wood-framed farmhouse. He saw a shotgun leveled toward him. He knew nothing after that. His family was left waiting for a man who would never return. I had promised myself that I would never allow work to become more important than family or, as in my father's case, life itself.

I reached the house and knocked. In small-town rural America, you never forget your manners. When no reply came, I assured myself that the suspect was in the barn, so I welcomed myself into the house. I pulled open the screen door and reached for the solid inner door. My hand slid off the doorknob. I backed up a step and took my mittens off. An officer's voice came through the dark. "No one in the barn. Check out behind." I was going to warm myself while they were busy slogging through the snow looking for a man presumed to be armed. The call was actually one of those nuisance kinds. A man discharging a firearm had upset neighbors with the noise. Such a call could mean anything from a drunken sot shooting at his empties to a heartbroken lover shooting at the moon.

With my father many years dead and buried deep in my memory, I twisted the doorknob, pushing it open. The rush of fear hit my stomach and bowels, but before they could empty their contents, my mind screamed obscenities and I reacted. From behind the door extended a rifle barrel. I slammed my shoulder into the door and continued banging the door against the man with the gun who stood behind the door. I wanted to push him and his gun through the wall and on into hell. I slammed the door again and again, screaming for the deputies. They came running, their guns drawn. I kept slamming the door and screaming, "He's here." The gun dropped but I wouldn't let the assailant fall. I kept bouncing him between the door and the wall.

After the arrest, when all was silent, I sat in my car, shaking, coming down from the adrenaline rush. I was driving home to my family. I then thanked my father for watching over me. I let the many years of anger toward him fall away with my tears of relief and remorse.

Gypsy Caravan

IT HAD BEEN a long day at work. I was managing a group home for delinquent boys. It had been a normal day, with the boys testing the limits of rules and staff patience. It had ended with staff and boys learning lessons. It had been a good day, a typical day. I poked my head into the living room to say goodbye to staff. The phone rang and I decided I could answer it as I left. It was the chief deputy. He asked if I could stop by the sheriff's office. They had a situation.

Situation means something bad. Even worse, I knew my dad was out of town. Situations never got "really bad" when he was around. I was heading into trouble. I pulled up at the sheriff's office and I noticed an unusual number of squad cars parked around the building. There were sheriff's cars, local police squads as well as highway patrol vehicles, and some cars from neighboring counties. It appeared something big was going down. Inside the lobby was a horde of children and young people. They all had beautiful black hair and dark olive skin. They stood out in a community of Scandinavian descendants. The children were accompanied by several adult women. Then a commotion in the inner offices caught my attention, and I saw six men who were obviously with this group gesturing wildly and shouting, "No English, no English," trying to indicate they could not communicate. I had an idea of the situation; I just wasn't aware yet of the particular circumstances.

Every spring and summer, bands of Gypsies came through southern Minnesota running scams and cheating the local "Gorgers." They traveled in large families. This group numbered more than twenty, and they traveled in three cars. Everything they needed was packed in the cars. That was part of the scam. How could small, rural law enforcement agencies deal with such numbers, especially when a dozen of them were children? Do you jail the adults and put the children in foster care? The logistics and expense were often beyond the resources of small communities.

Last summer a group of Gypsies had set up business at a campground in a community just across the county line. This was planned. They would not commit crimes in the county where they camped. They would travel beyond county lines to do "business" and return to their temporary homes, causing jurisdictional problems.

Typical scams were black-topping driveways or painting homes at rates that unsuspecting citizens could not turn down. With the next rain the worthless materials washed away. People were lucky if they only lost the investment in some labor and materials. Often the "job" was a good way to gain knowledge of the home and belongings. At times money and prized possessions would disappear with the withdrawal of jovial workmen.

My dad had gone to the Gypsy encampment last summer to retrieve some money for the good people of Waseca County. As he drove into the campground, his car was surrounded by dozens of pushing and shoving Gypsies curious as to why a single officer would come into their circle. My mom and youngest siblings stayed in the car. My dad got out into the swirling crowd and started walking. The children of the camp stayed near the car, staring at the strange people contained within the sheriff's car.

As my dad walked, the crowd would attempt to block his way. They jostled and pushed him as he tried to ask questions. No one spoke English. My dad knew what he was looking for. He had developed an uncanny amount of knowledge about people and cultures just from listening and paying attention to the many people he met. He was looking for the most expensive trailer in the encampment. He knew that Gypsy culture was matrilineal and that everyone in the camp answered to a queen, the woman in charge. The Gypsies were becoming nervous as they realized my dad didn't play by the rules. He wasn't going to ignore their trespasses. The pushing and shoving became more defensive and earnest. My dad just kept walking, asking questions, and continuing a one-sided conversation. When he found the trailer he was looking for, he walked up and with great authority pounded on the door.

An older woman answered who also spoke "no English." My dad spun her around and put handcuffs on her. He then announced to everyone as loud as he could that he was taking his prisoner to jail! This was sacrilegious. No one had ever been so ill mannered. An edge of danger was developing. My mom was getting very nervous. She wasn't sure Dad was going to make it back to the car. He had the old woman by the arm, and she was on her tiptoes trying to keep up with the pace my dad set as he angled for the squad car. At the car, my dad turned to the crowd. "Do you want to see her in jail?"

"No English" was the chant.

"I'm taking her to jail unless I have eight hundred dollars in my hand right now."

"No English, no English."

My dad opened the door to the backseat of his car and told the kids to move over. He put his hand on top of the old woman's head and set her into the backseat. He moved to open the driver's door. There was a loud commotion and a frenzy of activity. Eight hundred dollars was thrust into his hands.

"Son of a bitch cop." English was quickly reestablished.

GYPSY CARAVAN

The current situation had developed several hours before in Mankato. The adults in this family group had entered a grocery store. The women, in their multi-colored full-length skirts, had gone to the back of the store and created a near riot. When all store staff had run to assist in breaking up the melee, the men emptied the cash registers and the store safe. With a predetermined signal the women calmed down and met the men in the cars, and they made their getaway.

The whole crew was apprehended somewhere in Blue Earth County. When the officer recognized his dilemma, what to do with so many children, he decided to just escort them to the county line. This was usual procedure. Each county would escort these family groups to the next county until they were in another state, and then the problem became someone else's. I imagine what happened was on the exchange between Waseca and Blue Earth Counties, one of the Gypsies got mouthy or a new officer got overzealous, but now we had an office full of people, accused and accusers who had no idea how to mediate the situation. There were at least seven separate arguments happening in the sheriff's office. Each was louder than the next.

The children were doing what kids do, and the whole atmosphere was right out of *Circus Boy*. The chief deputy pulled me aside and asked me to take charge of the children. I believe his reasoning was that since I worked with adolescent boys, I had to be a

PLAYING COPS

specialist in child psychology.

The children ranged in age from two to twenty. They were milling around, casually interacting with each other and laughing at the adults. I began to interject myself into their conversations. The young kids spoke English very well, as did every one of them when no one was watching. As soon as I would start a conversation with a young child, an older child would walk over, and if a stern look didn't end the conversation, a slap on the back of the head did. For two hours I tried to be their friend. It was fascinating to watch the interactions. Sometimes a younger youth would forget themselves and use English, or they might be showing too much interest in me, and an older child would immediately put them in their place. It was all part of their culture. I was an outsider and not to be trusted.

It seemed no resolution was in sight. The cars and the men had been searched. No money was found. They women had voluntarily turned over groceries, including frozen meats that they had hidden in large pockets sewn into their long skirts. Still, the money was missing.

My dad finally came to the office. Without asking questions, he had the women and men separated. Everyone continued to deny they knew English and feigned they could not understand the orders. With some loud vocalizations and a little pushing, the women were placed into a large holding cell, where they could not hear or see the men. Then my dad called me into the inner office. He introduced me and told the men that I ran a special home for wayward youths and that I was going to take their children and they would not see them again unless they cooperated. He gave them no time to argue and discuss. He whispered in my ear, "Load them into the van and then drive around for a couple of hours."

So that's what I did. We drove around the lakes and stopped at the park to play. I even treated everyone to a root beer at the drive-in. We were getting along wonderfully well. Two hours passed and I packed them back into the van and returned to the sheriff's office.

The most important aspect of Gypsy culture is family. My dad did not even attempt to barter with the adults about the kids. He knew the men would be in desperate trouble with their wives for losing the children. He also knew that the adults would do anything to see the children returned. When I came back, a reunion occurred that you would have thought had embraced years of separation. Everyone was hugging and kissing and loudly proclaiming their love for each other...in English!

The adult Gypsies believed my dad was crazy enough to have swept their children away to never be seen again, and he may have even given them that impression. After much howling and consternation with the disappearance of their children, he had simply asked for all the money to be returned. The women

PLAYING COPS

were escorted one at a time by the jail matron (my mother), who asked them to reach into the deepest recesses in their bodies and pull out the packages of rolled-up dollar bills. My mom always seemed to get the dirtiest jobs.

Another day in the life of the sheriff's family had drawn to an end. I had eaten nothing since noon. My mom asked if she could make me a sandwich. I made sure she washed her hands first.

Hide and Seek

I REMEMBER SAYING to anyone who was listening, "I think he's over here." I said it in subdued tones. I didn't want to give away my fear. It wasn't the first dead body I had found, but it was one of the saddest. I had assumed from the beginning we would find something extraordinary. My father had recruited my younger brother Todd and me to assist him in looking for a missing person. He was only missing in that his bar stool had been empty for several days, and his friends had missed him on the third day. This was Todd's first body hunt. It was part of the coming-of-age process in our family. Todd was to make the leap from adolescence to adult this day. He was about to meet death in all its immediacy and gruesomeness.

We drove in silence to the home of the lost civilian. The stillness was disturbed only by the crackling of my dad's radio as he attempted to get a clear channel. These rides were numbingly exciting. Bodies to be found charged me with fear and anticipation. We had learned in these circumstances to encumber our emotions with silence.

The settling evening sky and the old graveled driveway led us through a canyon of junked cars. The rusting hulks were piled three and four high. My dad's car was clattering and shimmying through potholes and muddy ruts. Todd and I stared straight ahead. The dead cars piled sky high creaked and groaned. The only thing holding them together was their obsolescence and stark dysfunction.

The rutted road flowed through the rusted canyon and opened onto a small meadow. An old two-story farmhouse stared us down. It was slowly dying. Windows gaped like long-lost teeth, and paint peeled like open wounds. Small shrubs and plants weaved in and out of the foundation, eating away at the soul of the house.

We exited the car and followed a small path through knee-high grass to the front door. "Wait here," my dad quietly ordered. Todd and I stood at the bottom of creaking wooden steps. My dad tried the door and entered the darkness. He called for us to follow. We turned on our flashlights in the darkened halls. Dusk had descended and the dying structure beckoned us menacingly.

My dad called for the missing man. No response. Todd and I joined in a chorus but still no response. Even though this was a mission of mercy, I still felt like an intruder. The silence was unnerving. The anticipation of what might be was overwhelming. We continued calling out in fear. Only stillness answered. We divided up and began searching. We continued calling out, our voices cracking under the strain of pending death. The darkness, the stale air, the smell of death, the stench of a life lived free of hygienic concerns caused each step in this lair to be an exercise in bowel control. The sound of my beating heart plugged my ears and muffled the chirps of crickets inside.

We went in separate directions. My father took the stairs. I secretly hoped he'd be the winner of this scavenger hunt. Todd walked toward the back of the house and the kitchen. I took a left into what I presumed had been a living room. The neglected exterior of the house hid the greater decay of the interior. I kicked cans and bottles as I shuffled through the trash. Heaps of bundled newspapers created alleyways. My imagination saw bodies lying everywhere.

The house continued to echo with shouts of "Hello?" and "Is anyone home?" My flashlight went out. My eyes adjusted. In the dark, blood looks like shadows. A large shadow, a pooled shadow, embraced an old sofa. The syrupy liquid surrounded empty whiskey bottles. An outline on the couch took form. A small man lay rigidly upon the cushions. He appeared frozen. His dead body appeared to be pushing away from the couch. His open mouth screamed nothing. I caught my breath. A stain ran from his mouth. It pooled upon the couch and then cascaded to the darkened stream on the floor.

"Hello." No answer. I had discovered death. I froze for a second. Then a shiver overcame me. My stomach played hopscotch. My throat tightened. I choked out the first words. Then I tried again, more clearly. "He's over here." The family reunited in the silence of death. Todd, too, froze. My dad was too familiar with this scene. He became workmanlike. He went to the car and called for a hearse. Todd and I hadn't moved when he re-entered. "Are you okay?" My dad's words unfroze us. We felt we'd been given permission to breathe again. Todd and I went outside and looked at the stars. We waited in silence for the hearse.

We rode home in silence. The thousands of words and emotions that had swept over us were left at the scene, not to be spoken. It was an unwritten rule, fastidiously held to, that we never discussed these events. No one shared their inner screams. As we entered the town, the lights of the Dairy Queen shone bright. A cold body and cold treats ended the day.

Monsters in the Night

IT WAS A dark fall night. The wind was blowing, and lightning was flashing in the distance. A great storm was focused on finding us. Doug was six, I was five. We were telling the younger kids stories of great monsters as the trees moaned outside. Mom was chastising us for scaring the little ones. In the middle of one of Doug's best stories, we heard a car stop in front of the house. The door blew open with a great gust and a booming thunder. We leaned together for protection.

Behind a great clashing of lightning, we saw Dad standing in the doorframe blocking out the fury of the wind. He had his raincoat over his uniform. He took off his hat and shook rain to the floor. He looked our way and smiled, saying something silly. He then looked to Mom and nodded toward the kitchen. Doug and I were young, but we were already aware that important adult conversations happened in the kitchen when adults were alone.

We left our siblings in front of the TV and we

scooted and crawled toward the kitchen to better hear. Dad's voice was excited and very serious. He talked in heavy whispers, but we heard. A man my mother had known had escaped from the state hospital for the mentally ill. He was known to be dangerous. Dad was just alerting Mom to be cautious. He left, pulled out of the house by the secrets of the night. Mom quickly locked the door. She went back to the kitchen and locked that door. She then directed us all to bed and ushered the younger children toward their beds.

Doug went to the kitchen, and I heard him in the cupboards. I did as Doug did. He was my big brother. He had found a cast-iron frying pan. He stared at it as if to guess its heft. He saw me and handed me the black pan. His upper half disappeared into the cupboard. Pans banged against each other, and he emerged with a frying pan twice the size of the one he had just handed me. Doug looked very serious. I was scared. A bad man could be coming to hurt my mom.

The front entrance to the house was a small vestibule. A wooden bench was built into the wall. I followed Doug and we planted ourselves on top of the bench, each holding our blackened weapons. It seemed as if we sat the whole night. Doug didn't flinch. He was intense, staring at the door, daring any bad man to break in. Doug would deal with any uninvited guest swiftly. I know I dozed. My eyes were heavier than the weapons we held. Doug would

MONSTERS IN THE NIGHT

nudge me as I slid toward the floor. We kept watch. I was scared.

Sometime later Dad returned and gave Mom the all-clear. The dreaded demon that had walked the darkened night had been caught and returned to the hospital, ending our vigil. We put our pans down, got into our pajamas, and slept fitfully, for bogeymen walked in our dreams.

Dinner and a Show

WORK WAS HARD to find. I had a college degree but no employment, so I returned home for the summer following my graduation. The B.S. wasn't opening any doors, and I was banking on my parents to feed me. The summer was turning into fall, and lack of effort kept me from a promising career. I had been given a suitcase for a graduation gift; you would have thought a college grad would understand that unspoken message. To get rid of me, my dad found me a job at the Sheriff's Boys Ranch. Not a bad gig, I thought. How hard would it be to herd boys? Shifts were ten days on and five off. Sounded pretty sweet in the beginning, but after a few months of constant strife, if a boy asked for the salt toward the end of a ten-day shift, and even if he smiled while asking, he was toying with his life.

After a year a new opportunity presented itself. A joint venture between Waseca and Le Sueur Counties to develop a group home for delinquent boys was advertised. They needed a director, and I need a change

DINNER AND A SHOW

of pace. Only three people applied. I knew the other two. They were hometown folk right out of college. Due to a lack of choices, I was offered the job. It offered a multitude of challenges. The biggest one wasn't in the job description.

The board of directors I worked for was made up of county officials from Waseca and Le Sueur Counties. Board meetings rotated monthly between the two county seats. The meetings were generally held at nightclubs, and sometimes people over imbibed on beer and spirits, and the meetings would become quite a raucous show by the end.

Le Sueur County was hosting a meeting at the Little Dandy, a fine eating establishment with a full bar. The Le Sueur contingent was getting wound up early. The Le Sueur County sheriff was as mischievous and sly as my father. They both enjoyed a large laugh, and if it was at someone else's expense, all the better. The conversation eventually came around to the Le Sueur County probation officer who had wrestled in high school and had done fairly well. He was letting the liquor exaggerate his exploits. He talked big and the sheriffs encouraged his bravado. Like a small wind blowing into a cyclone, Pat Smith, the Le Seuer County sheriff, began to chide and taunt the probation officer to strut his stuff. My dad threw out the challenge. Let the little puffed-up man wrestle me. I had wrestled in college and outweighed my dinner mate by forty pounds. No way was this going to happen. The PO wasn't that drunk, we were in a crowded restaurant, and we were wearing suits. The sheriffs couldn't let go. They egged the probation officer on with taunts of a diminutive manhood. When he took the bait, they bolted up and were assisting diners to pick up their plates, tables, and children, and move. They pushed everyone and everything up against the walls, clearing the middle of the dining floor.

They stripped my drunken opponent to his briefs, and when their attention turned my way, I chucked my coat, shirt, and tie. The diners seemed a little confused. The sheriffs didn't notice and didn't care. They pushed me and my smaller opponent into the middle of the chaos. We shook hands and the match was on.

I started slowly, all too aware of the surroundings. My opponent, emboldened by drink and delusions of grandeur, charged at me. I caught him in a hip throw, and he sailed toward the floor, his foot clipping the edge of a table. Turf and surf flew. Steak, lobster, and my reddened opponent were lying prone.

The sheriffs lifted my arm in triumph. The meeting adjourned.

My Mother's Tears

I ONLY SAW my mother cry on two occasions. She had nine children and a husband who constantly put himself in harm's way. She would get frantic and she could become paranoid with worry, but she never cried. Fear registered easily on her face but never grief, until…

The county fair was in town. These were hectic times with my father working sixteen-hour days and more. Townspeople would get ripped off by the carnies, and the carnies would do battle with the revenging town folk. There were always people who spent too much time in the beer tent, and young women with nothing to gain and little hope would disappear behind the trailers and tents. Frantic and angry parents would come searching. Each year a different carnival arrived bringing the same problems.

My dad had just bought a new car. He had moved up to a sedan, so the family station wagon was an extra expense we didn't need. My father came home from the fair to catch a cat nap and have supper. Going out the door he looked over his shoulder and said, "One of the carnival guys wants to buy the wagon," and he was gone.

At eight o'clock that evening, my father returned sitting in the backseat of a city squad car. This was unusual. He never came home before dark and he never sat in the backseat. The squad rolled to a slow stop. My mom went to the door expecting trouble. Dad got out. He had a bundle in his arms. He slowly walked to the house as if he were carrying fine china. At the bottom of the stairs, he looked up to my mom and extended the bundle. She grasped in her arms an infant. She pulled the blanket from its face and peered down at a Native child with a large smile and fistfuls of black hair. She looked up and my dad was already entering the squad. He smiled and waved. "I traded the wagon for the baby," and he was gone.

He gave her the real story the next morning. He had sold the car. The buyer's wife had run away and left him with the infant. He couldn't take care of the baby on the road, and my father, ever the pragmatist, declared his family could take care of the baby until the carnival season finished and the father could return for the child.

After nine babies of her own, I would have assumed that the thought of caring for a stranger's child might have sounded like work. My mom treated the little one as if it were her tenth or even the first. She

MY MOTHER'S TEARS

would carry him around gently cooing. She patiently warmed his formula and cradled him when he cried. Our home had been a sanctuary for many children, and my mom was always able to keep her heart guarded for she knew that each child would soon be leaving. This time her heart was overwhelmed, and she bonded tightly to the little boy.

Six weeks later the father returned. He had reunited with his wife, and they had come to reclaim their prodigal son. The exchange was awkward. There were many great thanks, handshakes, and an extremely slow transfer of the baby from one mom's arms to another's.

With the newly reunited family disappearing down the driveway, my mother began to weep. Embarrassed, she went to her bedroom and remained there for many sorrowful hours. We walked around the house for weeks as if we were in the midst of a wake. The tears dried but her eyes would always moisten when my dad would tell the story of the time he traded a car for a baby.

Children were also involved the second time I saw her cry. These children, too, were youngsters of misfortune. My father once again had improvised and brought to our home and the welcoming heart of my mother children of sorrow.

My father had gone to a murder. A man had strangled his wife, leaving two children. The whole affair was a tragedy. The man was a simple man who loved his wife. His coworkers used his simplemindedness for their entertainment. They constantly teased him to get a reaction. They discovered that he did not deal well with the thought that his wife could be cheating on him. More pressure was applied, more lies were conceived, and the men laughed at the frenzied reaction of this simple man. The teasing went on for months. The man's frantic reactions turned to paranoia and rage, and he went home for lunch one day and killed his wife.

The children had been in school. When informed of the trauma, they were numbed. My dad brought them to my mother's strong arms, and they became her children. She fed them and washed them. She sat with them at night when the terror of loss and abandonment became too much. She held them huddled against her waist at the funeral. She sat with them at the jail so they could see their father. She provided the safe harbor they needed as they searched for new moorings.

Weeks later, relatives came for the children. My mom hugged them for the last time. She whispered goodbye to each child as they walked out the door, went to her bedroom, and grieved deeply. Tears for lost children flow unevenly.

People in High Places

WHEN I WAS young I remember my dad saying you could give Hubert Humphrey a nickel and he could talk about it all day. He meant it as a compliment. He was a big fan of the senator, and he didn't mind dropping his name, although I wasn't sure he had ever met the senator. The Rotary Club in Waseca had organized a father-and-son baseball trip to watch the Minnesota Twins play in the old Metropolitan Stadium. The seats were just okay. A pole hid some of the action. The game was in the third inning, and we had missed a couple of good plays. My dad nudged me and called on several of the group to follow. We met some usher, and the poor guy was led to believe that my father was a good friend of the senator's and "Hubert" had insisted we use his box for the game. I knew my dad had moxie, but I still wasn't convinced he'd even spoken a word with the senator. My dad could run a scam with the best con men. I often thought that was why he was so effective. He could shovel the bullshit faster and deeper than most of the con men he spent his life befriending, in different ways.

Some years later I was operating a group home for boys in Waseca, and my dad invited me to a meeting at his office. He and sheriffs from surrounding counties had received a drug enforcement grant from the federal government that they worked cooperatively on. A federal auditor was meeting with them to determine whether the grant should be continued.

What wasn't known to the fed was that these men, the sheriffs, were not only the definition of "good ol' boys," but they were the best of friends and worked so well together, the "bad guys" thought they were related by blood. They certainly were forged from the same metal. Statistically they had accomplished all the goals of the grant, and they were expecting cigars and pats on the back. Five minutes into the interview, the fed dropped the bomb: He couldn't advise continuing the grant as he wasn't sure these men were or could work cooperatively.

This was not going to be pretty. I envisioned the agent spending thirty days as a guest in each of at least four separate county jails. Heated debate erupted. I sat back greatly relieved that I wasn't going to be on the receiving end of this tongue lashing.

Then I noticed a most peculiar thing. My dad wasn't screaming. He was dialing the phone. Silence soon followed as each man in the room noticed my dad's off-handed behavior. He continued dialing.

PEOPLE IN HIGH PLACES

When he finished he sat back with a queer little smile. He covered the phone with his hand, leaned forward toward the federal agent, and very calmly asked if he'd like to change his opinion. "Last chance," he said, "or I'll have you shining shoes at the Radisson." The agent's back stiffened, but he didn't budge on his opinion.

"Hi, could I speak with Senator Humphrey" were the first words out of my dad's mouth. I was thinking this was going to be one tough scam to pull off. The agent held his ground. My dad continued, "Tell Hubert the sheriff is calling." He didn't say Sheriff Eustice, or the sheriff from Waseca County. He said "the sheriff." Wow, impressive. I had to see how he was going to run this one out.

He explained to someone on the phone the circumstances of the meeting and how this young agent had no concept of cooperative law enforcement. He handed the phone to the agent, "Senator Humphrey would like to speak with you," and he sat back and put his hands behind his head as if he was enjoying a great spectacle.

I could hear the senator's unmistakable voice burning through the wires. The agent turned a whiter shade of pale. He handed the phone back to my dad, who exchanged pleasantries with the senator and hung up. "You'll have my cooperation" was all the agent could say.

Porcelain Dolls

DOUG COLLECTS BEAUTIFUL porcelain dolls. They seem almost alive. They are finely detailed and all share pale white porcelain faces. They wear clothes so perfect and clean and remind me of past times when life seemed easier but was just as imperfect.

Doug was in his early teens when he was catching a ride with Dad to a part-time job. The radio came to life and the chatter began. Dad's dispatcher said that the train master had called; there had been an accident and a death in Otisco. Dr. Norman, the coroner, and the ambulance service had also been notified. Dad pressed the button that activated the siren, and he and Doug took a wild ride south to Otisco.

It was a midsummer day and the sun blazed on the corn and bean fields. Pollen filled the air and the faint scent of manure rode the breeze. A small crowd had gathered at the railroad crossing in the middle of Otisco. The silence of the gathering was deafening. Solemnity hung on everyone's shoulders, pulling faces forward and toward the ground. The ambulance arrived just behind Dad and Doug. Dr. Norman got out and walked with Lyle, the ambulance owner. All conversations were held in hushed tones. People were crying and holding each other. Some were awkwardly pointing down the tracks, embarrassed that others might see them gawking at the sight of death.

Dad asked the crowd to disperse and gently pushed people back toward their cars. Those who had witnessed the accident and the parents remained. The story that was stitched together was tragic. Two teenage sisters were walking to town on this warm summer day to get a soda and some candy. As they came to the tracks, they saw the train, which was blowing its whistle, sending out its universal warning. The girls had stopped and then suddenly one bolted. She had gotten across and turned and motioned for her sister. The younger girl had hesitated. The older girl turned back as the younger girl stepped forward. The train hit them both. The engineer said there was a sickening thud.

One girl's body lay covered near the intersection. The second body had been thrown about seventy feet down the tracks. She lay in a deep ditch—obviously dead. Dr. Norman, aged and infirmed, didn't think he could climb down the grade, so Doug was sent to retrieve the body.

Doug walked the tracks until he stood over the site of the girl's body. He was surprised how peaceful she looked. She appeared to be sleeping. She was small with long, dark, curly hair. Death had painted her skin a pale white. Her neck had been broken, and her head appeared oddly placed. Doug decided to carry her back to the intersection to her waiting parents and the ambulance. He gently pulled her to his chest and quietly walked back to the crowd and her waiting parents. He laid her gently onto the ambulance stretcher. Hair covered her eyes, so he carefully brushed it aside. He stepped back to allow the mourners near for their goodbyes. He caught his breath, stuffed his emotions, and walked back to the car and sat.

My brother collects porcelain dolls.

You Don't Tug on Superman's Cape

RICHARD K. WAS a known entity in New Richland. He was known to be a little crazy. He was known to drink hard, and he was known to be dangerous. He was living lousily in New Richland. Friends took him in occasionally, feeling sorry for the disoriented man, only to be forced to call the police to escort Richard out after he had overstayed the average man's sense of sanity. It was getting cold. Snow twirled in the early evenings, prepping for the big fall. When doors wouldn't open for him, and he was forced into the late fall night alone, he would buy a bottle of Wild Turkey and curl up with Sam, his German shepherd. The good shepherd and the psychotic Turkey would keep Richard warm in the backseat of a beaten-down '62 Pontiac.

Richard had few friends and fewer interests. A good night was drinking to the brink of an animal fury and then driving around town shooting out streetlights and screaming vulgarities at people and enemies imagined and real.

He got into his routine on a Friday night when a part-time cop, fresh from the Marines and Nam, decided to return fire. He fired eight times at Richard, who managed to stagger between bullets and, catching a sane moment, realized his days of menacing the street department of New Richland could prove fatal.

He headed north on Highway 13 toward the county seat. He drove drunk and he drove fast. He knew in his delirium if he stayed too long on the blacktop, he'd be arrested. So he drove hard to outrun any potential arrests. He got to Waseca around 10 p.m. At the stoplight, he fumbled in his glove compartment and found a bottle and his gun. He slugged the rest of the whiskey and rolled down the side window. Grace lit up his face. A fresh street filled with bright and abundant streetlights. He pulled away from the stoplights slowly, not wanting to attract attention, and lined his car up with the center line on the road so as to avoid parked cars. Then he moved forward, assaulting the rows of new streetlights.

The Waseca cops weren't retired; they just acted that way. Day or night, they drove their cruiser to the quietest streets to catch a few nods, but bullets couldn't be ignored. They slowly but surely started toward the sound of the ensuing battle. Two squads cut Richard off. Richard cursed and stumbled out to confront the Blue goons. An inglorious battle ensued, and Richard was subdued and arrested.

Waseca was between jails. The century-old stone structure had been demolished to give way to a new brick-and-steel building. Only footings for the new structure existed. The sheriff's department had retreated to a small cement block building behind the old jail. New arrestees were taken to the annex to be processed and then they would be transported to Owatonna for more permanent residency.

Four cops escorted Richard into the annex and, feeling smug, they took his handcuffs off. Who knows what happens to people too crazy or too drunk to know they're outnumbered. Sometimes they step into an invisible phone booth and come out Superman. Richard pushed the booking deputy to the floor and then used the twenty-by-fifty-foot building as his own private gym, climbing walls, throwing furniture, and assaulting any patrolman who dared to come into his reach.

Quickly bruised and battered, the cops retreated to the door and decided if they couldn't regain control of Richard, they'd at least block his escape. Needing reinforcements they called my family's home. They told my mother that they had been in contact with my father and that he wanted Doug, my brother, to come up to the annex and quiet Mr. K down.

Doug was a quiet soul, a gentle soul, but he had been born with monstrous strength. When we were young and in Boy Scouts, the troop would play "king of the hill." Doug would claim the hill and the troop would attack. We all could have earned our Air Wings in those fights. It really wasn't fair. Doug outmuscled us. We always lost miserably.

Doug got to the annex. He pushed past the officers to get inside. Richard was in great form. He ran from office to office screaming at the devils in his head and throwing everything in his reach. He was a man on fire. Doug took off his jacket and placed it on the booking desk. Richard smiled—he was six foot, over two hundred pounds, and he had just beaten back the Waseca Police Department, and now they send in some punk-ass high school kid. Richard bent over and started digging down inside the pipe of his cowboy boot. Doug moved forward, and Richard stood up straight and rushed toward Doug to bowl him over. Doug caught him by the throat with his right hand, his strong hand. With a lifting and twisting motion, he slammed Richard's head against the wall, and with his left hand, he reached to the desk and grabbed a pair of handcuffs. He left Richard dangling for a minute or two, Richard choking for air. He went limp and Doug put the cuffs back on Richard's slack arms. He threw Richard into an office chair and rolled him to the front door.

Mert, the chief deputy, had made an appearance. His squad car sat just outside the door, engine running for the trip to Owatonna. Richard, slurring his words, offered to behave himself and to walk to the car. He stood and then rushed Mert; Doug threw a shoulder into Richard's middle. The air flew from his stomach like a balloon bursting. Doug hung him over his shoulder, walked to the car, and threw Richard toward the backseat. He missed the first time, and Richard's head bounced off the roof of the car. Doug's aim improved on the second attempt. Doug said Richard was more compliant the second time. Richard complained to Mert that Doug had hurt his throat and his singing voice. He started to warble. Mert suggested he keep his mouth shut and his pipes would heal. Doug rode shotgun to Owatonna. When the Owatonna police patted Richard down, they found a knife in his boot. Luckily he didn't pull the knife on Doug; he might have made Doug mad. You might chance tugging on Superman's cape, but you never wanted to make Doug mad.

Runaways

THE FIRST TIME I ran away from home, I had money in my pocket and a beautiful redhead on my arm. It was an impulsive act. I wasn't rebelling, nor was home life hell. I just needed to be on the move. It was a gorgeous July morning with huge billowing white clouds forming castles in the sky and the sun bringing everything to life, including my adventurous spirit.

I was headed downtown to spend money on my girl. The street was lined on both sides by huge stately elms. They formed a canopy that allowed us to walk in shade all the way to the business district. Birds in the higher branches sang as we walked. Insects chirped in the grass. It was glorious and I took my girl's hand. We squeezed our hands and held on tight. We were rapidly walking into a great adventure.

She was animated. She talked faster than anyone I had ever known. She could squeeze into five minutes a lifetime of conversation. She chattered constantly, out singing the crickets. I didn't mind. It was all music to me and I just had to nod my head occasionally to keep her engaged.

There were lots of kids in yards and adults out for walks. The sidewalks were works of chalk art. We came to the marking of a hopscotch game, and she challenged me. I never understood the foot work, and she laughed as I twisted and fell. I jumped back up and ran ahead, calling back to her, "Don't step on any cracks, you'll break your mother's back." Giggling and smiling in her special way, she caught up.

We turned off the avenue and found ourselves on State Street. The busy road was the heartthrob of the small community. Cars pushed each other for right-of-way. People walked hurriedly and purposefully. It was lively for mid-morning. The clock on the courthouse began to ring the hour. I grabbed my girl's hand again and we ran past the Busy Bee Café on our way to the dime store. We were two storefronts from the café when the sun was blotted out by a huge shadow and a voice sounding like thunder. "Gary, where do you think you're going?"

I didn't have to turn around. I knew the voice. My girl squeezed my hand as she turned. "There's your dad." Busted. My father stood in his blue patrolman's uniform. He had been drinking his morning coffee in the restaurant, and someone pointing had said, "Look at those cute children." My dad was on his feet and out the door. He was trying not to laugh. "Where's Mom?"

"At home," I said authoritatively.

"What are you doing here?"

I pulled the pennies out of my pocket and showing them to my dad, I said, "We're going to get candy."

He walked us to the dime store, and we got candy out of the big penny jars. He asked to use the store phone and called our mothers to let them know we were safe. He then put us in a taxi and sent us homeward, my girl and me. We were three years of age, and we had been on the run.

Scott

SCOTT WAS MY parents' third son and fourth child. A friend once told me that he believed my brothers and I were fearless. I encouraged him not to confuse courage with hard-headedness. In a family of single-mindedness, Scott was singularly minded. He was a working fool. He always had a job. He never seemed to be home but was always at work somewhere. He didn't have as many adventures as the rest of us in our youth playing deputy, but he became a real one as an adult. The single-mindedness he demonstrated as a young man carried him into law enforcement.

The summer following his high school graduation, he worked as a night attendant at a gas station on the west end of town. It had been an exceedingly hot, sticky, late July day. The night wasn't cooling off very quickly. The buildings and streets radiated heat that scorched and soaked everyone who was out and about. I drove into the station in the early evening on my way to pick up some friends. I got gas and gave my little brother a rash of big brother grief. He never found me funny. He would huff and give me a sly little grin to say "Get a job and be useful."

The station stayed open until the wee hours of the morning to catch all the drunks leaving the bars. Scott was in for another hot, boring, and lonely night. As the evening painfully dragged on, Scott took a break about eleven and went into the men's room. He hurried and got back to the till, as he was the only employee in the building, stationed himself behind the counter, and once again began counting cars as they drove by. He was deep into the meditation when a voice said, "Get your hands up; this is a robbery." Scott looked in the direction of the voice—from behind a rack of magazines, a gun was pointed at him. The voice deepened and became more serious. "Put your hands up." Scott felt for the loaded shotgun that was kept under the counter. He released the safety as the voice commanded once again, "Get your hands up where I can see them." As Scott started to pull the shotgun toward himself, he thought he might have recognized the voice. He let go of the gun and grabbed a bag of potato chips and hurled them at the would-be robber. A city cop stepped out and showed himself, snorting a large horselaugh. Scott shook his head thinking *What a dumbass*. The cop never knew how close he had come to dying. He walked outside to the squad he'd hidden on the side of the building, laughing how he'd pulled a big one. Scott shook his

SCOTT

head again and blew the incident off, still thinking, *Dumbass*.

Scott got back into the rhythm of dullness. Shortly after midnight a young lady walked in who was obviously wasted on a concoction of too many drugs and too much alcohol. She had trouble standing and used everything and anything handy to hold herself up. Scott recognized her as a former classmate. He had once sat across the aisle from her in a class. She had dropped out of school early. Scott realized he had never missed her, but he was feeling some compassion for her as she weaved her way up to the counter. She stood swaying, trying to focus her eyes, then pulled out a knife and pointed it at Scott. "Give me some money."

Scott laughed at her feeble attempt. "No, I can't do that. Just leave. Go home." She made a slow-motion attempt to lunge at him with the knife. He took it out of her hand. Laughing gently he put his face near her so she could focus. "Go home before you get into trouble."

She caught her balance. "I want some money."

"Sorry," Scott said, "not tonight." He came out from behind the counter and walked her out the door to the street and watched for traffic as she staggered across the road and off into the dark.

The night returned to its orderly, monotonous ways. A car came into the station drive going a little too fast, and as it passed between the large station windows and the pumps, I rolled down the window of a friend's car and mooned Scott. I thought it would break the boredom and give him something to talk about. I waited for him to get off his shift. When he came home, I asked how the night was. He just huffed and said, "Some jerk hung his butt out of a car window." He gave me that little sly grin and walked off to bed.

Shadow Dancing

I'VE ALWAYS BELIEVED I would die young. My father died when he was forty-six. I'm creeping up on fifty-nine, and I can't shake the feeling that I'm approaching some mystical milestone in my life, that somehow I'm living on borrowed time. My father was the single greatest influence in my life. I feel our lives are still intertwined. As a kid I idolized him and followed him around as much as he would allow. His sheriff's uniforms and his gold badge made him my hero. As an adolescent I began to see the cracks in his armor. I would go to public assemblies with him and find his speech patterns and mannerisms embarrassing. Now when I speak publicly I catch myself—or is it him?—for I hear the same inflections in my voice, and I use the same hand gestures as he, and when I catch myself, I smile with amusement.

He wore the brown uniform that represented social conservatism, but his heart bled the bright red blood of liberalism. He was forever bringing home the lost, the misbegotten, the misdirected, the abused, and the homeless. They stayed for a meal, a day, a week, sometimes for months. He spent as much time finding people shelter, work, food, and self-respect as he did enforcing the law.

I've walked in his shadow. Like him I have struggled to balance my private life with my work. More than thirty years dead, his shadow still crosses mine. A middle-aged woman chose me for her therapist. She recounted a story of childhood sexual abuse and a lifetime of heroic battles containing her pain.

She came to me because her contained sorrows had erupted again. She had seen me at meetings and heard me speak. Her words conveyed to me an unknown bond connecting the two of us by the long shadow of my father's life. "When you spoke I heard your father's voice. I chose to speak to you because you are your father's son. I trusted him and I want to trust you."

As a child she had been taken from her home on a northern reservation and placed in foster care in Waseca. She was physically and sexually abused by the adults who were entrusted with her care. She rebelled, but her behaviors were not seen as a cry for help; they were regarded as delinquent. She shared with a judge and social workers her abuse, but they labeled her a liar without investigating.

When she was twelve she began running away. She was easily caught each time she ran. She would

SHADOW DANCING

be brought to my father's jail. He had no knowledge of her abuse; he just saw a little girl lost. Against convention he would keep her in jail for several days following a run. She told me this with a smile. As a guest of the Waseca County jail, she received regular visits from my father for long talks. My mother would make her special meals, and my parents took turns at night reading to her. She came to see the jail as her sanctuary, her safe place.

She shared that she accompanied my dad to the social services department after one of her adventures. She was left in the waiting room while my dad walked to an office with several workers. She did not remember what was said; she just recalled that his voice was loud, commanding, and scary. All the social workers came scurrying out of the office, and she found herself on her way home to northern Minnesota on that very day. She had chosen me as her therapist because I reminded her of my father. She heard my words but his voice. She was in my presence, but she saw his mannerisms and gestures. We, the two, had become one.

My father only exists as a collection of memories and stories. Those fragments of his life have forged a large piece of my personality. They have molded and sculpted me. As I look back on that creation, I look forward to my eventual death. Someday I will exist only as the mist of memories and stories. Will the shadows of my life invade and meld into the lives of my children? After my death, will I foreshadow the lives of those who follow? I will never know. I would want my children to receive from me the gifts my father left: strength of conviction, courage to go beyond, respect for all, grace in humor, and an uncompromising love for those who struggle. I have nothing more valuable to give them than the extended shadow of their grandfather.

Shadows

LUNCH HAD STARTED when I slid my plate into the middle of a conversation. As I reached for the pepper, my colleague to the right was stating flatly that she never traveled without taking a handgun. Someone asked if she thought she could really use it. Without hesitation she declared, "If I thought my life was in danger, I wouldn't think twice."

I swallowed a bit of salad and thought, *Oh, really*.

My dad was the sheriff in a small rural county with an even smaller budget. Instead of paying his deputies overtime, he often gave my teen brothers and me long hours of duty at no expense to the county. The first time he handed me a gun, I was eighteen.

The FBI had informed us that a professional band of thieves from the metro area was going to attempt to steal a semi-trailer load of farm equipment. The feds knew when but not where. A three-county area was put on alert. These thieves were known to be armed and dangerous.

PLAYING COPS

I was teamed with an older and more experienced deputy. Ed and I were assigned an implement dealer in a neighboring county. The dealership was just off the freeway and a prime target. Ed drove and I nervously attempted conversation. Small talk is hard when testosterone and adrenaline are screaming for attention.

We arrived at our target site. We scouted the area and decided to park in a cemetery, on a hill, overlooking the machinery lot. In the wee morning hours as the chilled dew was beginning to blanket everything, a single car circled the dealership. The car parked in a grove of trees, and a man climbed over the chain-link fence surrounding the lot and disappeared into the rows of tractors and combines.

We radioed in. Like a hurricane, a dozen squad cars descended on the dealership and a dozen officers drew their guns. We entered the lot, and a single officer stood at the head of each row of machinery. Walking down the rows in unison, alone, we were like pheasant hunters flushing their quarry.

I took out my revolver, cocked it, pointed it toward the brilliant stars, and began a cautious, deliberate walk into the unknown. My nerves were on fire. My eyes darted from shadow to shadow. I was seeing movement everywhere. As I searched, I felt like the hunted.

Something moved. A faint sound of breath being released caught my ear. I brought my gun down. I tensed my trigger finger and pointed the gun into the darkness. A figure came running at me. I froze. My brain was screaming to fire. The figure stopped. I stood. The shadowy man came into the murky light and surrendered.

On a dark and dangerous night, a company mechanic had decided to steal a battery from his boss. He had no idea how close he had come to dying. I did.

While the other officers joked and laughed off their nervousness, I walked into the remaining darkness and threw up. The curdles of partially digested milk marked the spot where I could have killed a man. He was alive because in an instant of a second, I learned I could not pull the trigger.

The End of Summers

THE SUMMER OF 1976 was coming to a quick end. The late August weather had been typical for southern Minnesota: the days were hot and humid and the nights cooled rapidly. Labor Day weekend was approaching, and I had nothing in particular to do, so when my dad asked me to take on a stake-out, I agreed. Friday evening, I went to the family home to get my instructions. My dad was planning on taking the family to the Renaissance Festival the next day. Dad and Mom were talking out the plans for Saturday. Dad said he needed to serve papers on a relative the next day and then they could leave. Mom was a little steamed. Dad had sent a deputy who had failed to locate Kenny. Mom didn't like that my dad was always picking up after his employees.

Kenny was a distant relative. He farmed and every fall the stress of the harvest would trip his mental illness and he would need to be hospitalized. It came on very fast this fall. On Thursday, Kenny had come into the sheriff's office with a box of vegetables for his friend Don, my dad. They had chatted and Kenny seemed relaxed. On this Friday, his family had called and said that he was very paranoid and acting strangely. They felt it was time for Kenny to be hospitalized. A deputy had driven out, but Kenny wasn't located. Later Kenny would testify that when the deputy had arrived, he was in the barn with a rifle pointed at the deputy. Kenny had made up his mind if the deputy touched his dog, he was going to fire. The deputy knocked on the door, went to the back and knocked, and then left. That meant the following day, Saturday morning, Kenny needed to be taken to the hospital. My dad had decided to work it in before the family trip.

My father was sitting in *his* chair with a leg draped over the armrest and holding his chin in his right hand as if he were contemplating the world's problems. He had decided this was his last term as sheriff. He was talking with friends about his retirement from law enforcement and exploring what he wanted to do with the rest of his life.

I pulled a chair out from the kitchen table and sat down facing him. "What's up?" I got my instructions. The local lumber mart was being broken into on a regular basis. Someone was helping themselves to lumber out in the yard. It was thought it might be an employee, but who knew. I was planning for a long and boring night. Unless I got lucky and some fool decided to play the odds and return. Most stake-outs from my experience were extremely tedious. It usually called for long hours of fighting off sleep and trying to stay alert just in case. The last time out I watched a farm home for signs of drug sales. I walked across a half-mile-long field and crawled into a barn several hundred feet from the house and watched the activity at the house through cracks in the barn siding. It was believed the occupants were selling drugs and supposedly armed to the teeth. The excitement of possible action dissolved into extreme lethargy as I sat and sat noting nothing. I was nodding off to dreamland when I got whacked upside the head. I thought I might die. I caught myself, not screaming, but when I wheeled around, I saw it was a full-time deputy who had come to replace me. I could have kicked his ass, and I should have.

I had my assignment. I grabbed a Coke from the fridge and was heading for the door when my dad called me back. He went into his bedroom and came out with a snub-nosed .38. He never carried a gun. He sometimes kept one locked in the trunk or glove box of his car. He didn't like the image weapons put out. He would rather talk someone into obedience than threaten them. He was full of blarney and could talk anyone into just about anything. He handed me the gun. "Here, you never know when you might need one." This was most likely the second time I had ever been handed a weapon. I took it to mean he knew I was mature enough not to use it unless necessary. I put it in my pocket and headed home for a few hours of sleep.

I slept until midnight. The sky was clear and the moon bright. I wouldn't need a flashlight. Anyone moving around the lumber yard tonight would be clearly seen. I got to the yard, parked my car at another business a half mile away, and walked back. Finding a perch that gave me a good view of the surroundings, I settled back for a long night. I couldn't make any noise and I couldn't be seen. I sang the current top twenty to myself several times. I counted the stars. I made up stories. I dreamed of girls I had known and would like to meet. About three thirty a car drove in, but it quickly turned around and left. I got up and walked around a bit. The humidity made the night air chilled. I found an old tarp and wrapped myself up. I shivered for several minutes. Five a.m. came slowly. When it arrived, I decided enough was enough and started for home. I was really sleepy, so I stopped at my parents' home and lay down on the couch. My dad was the first to stir. I decided I wouldn't get much sleep from that point on, so without saying a word, I got in my car and went home.

Home was an old farm house I shared with several friends about ten miles from town. They had steady girlfriends, so the house was empty when I got there. I had pushed aside the tiredness and walked around the yard looking at the shine of the morning dew on different plants. The sun had broken not too long ago, but you could tell it was going to be a hot one. I remembered the gun in the car. I hadn't shot a gun much and thought *Why not?* I emptied the six shots at an old tool shed. I reloaded and destroyed a pile of old cans and bottles. I was surprised how the gun kicked. The need to sleep had returned, so I put the gun on the table next to the staircase and went up to my room and kicked all the covers onto the floor. It was going to be miserably hot.

Hot it was and the flies kept buzzing me. I was thrashing about, catching slim slivers of sleep; constantly being interrupted by the insect air command and my own sweat. Somewhere in this alien dance, I heard a distant gunshot. I rolled over thinking I deserved that. I had the passing thought some farmer had decided to pay me back for my six-gun salute earlier in the morning. The buzzing was deafening, and my angry sleep was so difficult to corral. I was falling in and out of slumber. The day was turning into one big headache. Then the phone began ringing. I had told some friends I'd join them at a softball tournament. I was too tired to get up and answer the phone. I thought they'd have the good sense to leave me alone after a couple of calls, but they just wouldn't give up. Ringing, buzzing, sweating, and more ringing. I went to the phone to plead with whomever to just leave me alone.

When I picked up the receiver, I was surprised to hear the voice of my mother's friend Ruth. "Gary, you need to come home. You're needed at home. There's been a family emergency." She may have had to repeat it a couple of times. With the little sleep I had gotten, I felt hung over. I just reacted. I pulled on the clothes from the night before and glanced at the clock as I ran out the door. It was only 11 a.m. In my head it seemed much later. I threw gravel flying down the driveway. I was trying to discern what Ruth meant by a family emergency. I thought maybe my dad had suffered a heart attack. Then I thought about my grandmother, in her eighties; she may have died. Either event was an emergency, and I pushed the gas pedal down. The road dipped down to a railroad crossing and immediately climbed up again. I hit it hard and became airborne on the upside. The road ran up and intersected with the main highway into town. The stop sign was clearly visible on approach. I looked to my left and the field was beans, which allowed a good view of coming traffic. I caught the wheel and hit the brakes. I fishtailed onto the blacktop and sped toward home as Steppenwolf was singing "Born to Be Wild." I felt insane.

In town I hung just above the speed limit and rolled through stop signs. I pulled up to the back door of my parents' place. Doc Norman and my sister Peggy were standing just to the side of the door. I was looking at Doc when Peggy's scream split my soul. "Dad's dead. Dad was shot." I don't know what registered, but I turned to my car screaming "Fuck" to no one in particular and kicked in the passenger door. I turned to catch Peggy in my arms. She wept for mankind, and through snot and tears wailed on about Dad being murdered. I don't remember how I disengaged, but I found myself in the house facing my mother. She seemed drained of life. She had been crying heavily. Her eyes and face drooped with the weight of a thousand tears. Her soul seemed to have soured. She stared at me blankly. Ruth was there. She was trying to tell me the facts. I hugged my mother, hoping my strength would return her to life. She was frozen. I pulled her to a chair, and we just stared at each other.

Facts and stories were whirling about in the emotional maelstrom. What I gathered was my dad had gone to Kenny's with his chief deputy, and Kenny had somehow killed him. Later the details would become clear. My dad had driven into Kenny's yard with his deputy. My dad was driving. Kenny had been encased in his paranoia. He had stood at the door of his kitchen all night. He screamed at his family that the devil was coming to get him. The car rolled to a stop. My father was dressed in his civilian clothes, ready for the family trip. His shirt was a wild print. Kenny could be seen standing behind the screen door in his kitchen. My dad took two steps toward the house. "Hi Kenny." Kenny stepped out, lowered his shotgun, and killed my father instantly. The wild print became a muddled red and purple. Mert Schwartz, my dad's deputy, yelled to Kenny, "You've killed Don!"

"No, I killed the devil" came Kenny's confused response.

I asked what I could do. My mom directed me to find her mother and bring her to the house before she heard the news from some other source. My younger brother Todd and I drove over to my grandmother's. She came to the door and invited us in. I asked her to sit down. She loved my father and I feared a terrible breakdown. When she had been seated, I told her the truth directly. She looked at me for only a second, and without any emotion said, "I'll get my hat." I was puzzled by her steadfast reaction. Later I came to believe that she had seen death so frequently, it was a trusted companion, no longer anything to be feared. Or maybe, like all good mothers, she needed to be with her child.

Nothing was said on the way to the house. Grandma adjusted her hat. Todd looked blankly out the window. We rolled to a stop and I dropped my passengers off and yelled at Todd I'd be back in ten. I drove three blocks and knocked on the door of my girlfriend's home. I was supposed to have a date later that day. I was just going to tell her I'd be delayed. Anne answered the door. She seemed startled to see me or maybe I wasn't looking so good. I stared at her face, afraid to allow her to see the pain in my eyes. I then fell to my knees and placed my head on her stomach, and the wail of the banshees flooded our ears. She held me close and I wept. I wept for my mom, I wept for my dad, and I wept for my family. I pushed myself away and told Anne I'd be with my family. I backed away in deep grief and more deeply ashamed of my tears. I must have looked like a child. They would be the last tears I'd shed that day.

My brothers and sisters were scattered around the state. They were checking in and getting the cold details. A continuous parade of well-wishers came to the door. Neighbors, friends, relatives, and felons, they all came to pay their respects. Everyone was stunned. They all leaned on each other for fear of life without the sheriff. The tears that flowed that day could have ended a western drought.

The day went by in a haze. Funeral plans were made, adjusted, pushed aside, and reinvented. Doug and Scott finally arrived. We sat in silence. Anger burned with the tears. I don't know who had the idea, but it was only put forth once and we acted. Kenny was in jail, our jail! He was going to answer to us. I don't know what was in their hearts, but mine beat cold and black.

There was a small crowd in front of the jail when we arrived. It appeared to be a pilgrimage. People silently stepped aside when they recognized us. We entered the jail and the dispatcher immediately buzzed us in. He came out of the control room, and he and the jailer led us to the cell block. In retrospect we were a common sight at the jail. We were a part of the

THE END OF SUMMERS

office. We had grown up with these men, and there was a bond and trust based on years of having each other's backs. We had been to the dark side together. The evil we knew and had faced together had made us peers; we were all deputies, all members of the sheriff's posse.

We were led down the aisle between cells until we came to the one which held my father's murderer. The jailer unlocked the cell door, then turned and left my brothers and me alone, face-to-face with the man I wanted to kill. I don't know what my brothers' intentions were at that moment, but anger and revenge had brought me to this spot. I stepped into the cell and slid along the wall to allow my brothers in.

In the far corner a small naked man cowered. He had no awareness of us. His fear and battles were with enemies unseen. He cried and whimpered and shouted at the demons that had possessed him. He looked frail and vulnerable, like a wounded child. We were frozen by his pain and were all looking at our feet. Nothing was said; we just turned in unison and walked out. The steel door clanged as I closed it. It must have startled Kenny as there was a brief moment of silence, and then the wail of a soul on fire burned through the jail.

It was Labor Day weekend. Dad died on Saturday morning, and we buried him on Labor Day. At times it seemed as if everything was in slow motion, but then it went by so quickly and we were faced with placing him in the ground.

The church brought the community together. Every pew was full and people stood quietly filling every inch of the holy building. Leaving the church the sky appeared streaked through my tears. The street was full of people. I wished to embrace them all. I held my mother and took her to the waiting cars. We drove deep into the country. My father's family had farmed. We were headed to a small country church and a graveyard that would be consecrated with the body of the man who had created me. A man I alternately had loved and feared. We were returning him to the soil from which he had sprung.

I helped my mother out of the car and put my arm around her as we hesitantly moved to the grave side. The church and graveyard stood on a small hill that allowed us to look back toward town. We could see miles of headlights floating toward us, led by dozens of squad cars from around the state, their red lights flashing. A great army of comfort moved toward us. The squad's lights framed a community's love. It was embracing. I held my mother a little closer, a little tighter.

Nothing was ever the same after that. That Labor Day was the end of summers.

The Family Car

SUMMER NIGHTS COMING home from visiting friends or relatives meant lying in the back of the station wagon and listening to the hum of the wheels and allowing the rhythm of the road to rock me to sleep. My dad tended to buy station wagons. Whatever the make of the car, it had to be a chameleon. Sometimes it just took care of the family, other times it became the sheriff's car, and at other times it was an ambulance or hearse.

It wasn't uncommon to be out for a leisurely family drive when my father would get a call or some dunce would pull some stupid traffic maneuver right in front of us. My dad would then pull down the windshield visors with attached flashing red lights and activate the siren underneath the hood, and the family outing would become a wild chase and a traffic stop. Later he added a large magnetic red light that he placed on the roof and plugged into the cigarette lighter. The effect was the same; the family car became super chase car.

PLAYING COPS

Getting to use the car was special, and its special powers were alluring. I took the car on a date to the Twin Cities. I had doubled with another couple, and we were heading home on the freeway. A car pulled up next to me, which I took as a challenge. I pushed the accelerator. He'd catch up. I pushed a little harder. He'd catch up. We jockeyed for position for a good twenty miles, hitting speeds in extreme excess of the speed limit. I was winning the race when the car challenging behind me began to honk his horn. The male driver motioned for me to roll down my window and he did the same. I thought he was going to issue a challenge, but I got a question. "Hey, Eustice, does the old man know you have the car?" He flipped his billfold open to show a badge. He sped off laughing harder than he was driving.

Blood runs were an adrenaline freak show. When blood was needed, a call would go out statewide. If blood needed to be transported, law enforcement would deliver it from one county border to the next. Waseca sat between Mankato and Rochester, the major medical centers in southern Minnesota. To get to make a blood run was wet-your-pants fun.

Todd and Barry were asked to take the car and fill it with gas. As they sat at the gas station, the car radio blared, "Sheriff's office to Car One." We had been drilled not to answer the radio. The dispatcher called out officially twice more. The boys knew better than to pick up the mike. Then he came back louder and

THE FAMILY CAR

with a little laughter in his voice. "Todd, your old man says you can answer." Dad came on the radio and told Todd to drive to the Blue Earth County line and pick up some blood being transported by a highway patrolman. "Todd, this is not an emergency; no need for the lights or siren." Todd turned the car out onto the highway and hit the siren. He was hitting eighty miles an hour before the city limits. The car tore through the countryside like a bullet on steroids. When they approached the town of Janesville and its red light on Main Street, Todd added the lights and siren and slowed down to seventy. When he was sure of making it through the lights, he punched it hard. Sidewalk pedestrians only saw two young faces flash by with frozen expressions of fear and delight.

Five miles from Janesville Todd spotted the highway patrol pulled off to the side. He raced to the parked squad and slammed on the brakes as he cranked the wheels and slid across the highway, ending up behind the patrolman. The cop got out looking confused. He pushed his hat back as he approached Todd with the blood. "I didn't know this was an emergency," he said, curiously.

"I was told it was," Todd responded and sent gravel flying as he took off homeward bound.

The car provided many new awakenings. We learned to drive in it. At sixteen a car and driving opened a vista of new opportunities. I took friends to Blue Earth to scout a football game. We got caught

PLAYING COPS

up in chatting with the local beauties. We had a large gang of young toughs decide that they were going to teach the outsiders a good lesson. Three carloads of angry adolescents chased us through the streets of Blue Earth. They had us boxed in, so I turned on the siren and continued racing through town. The policemen of Blue Earth stopped us, and when they learned of our plight, they gave us an escort out of town. Once safe we were still late for our curfews back home, so once again we hit the lights and siren and flew home.

The lessons the car brought were usually exciting and fun. Not always. On a late Saturday afternoon, I was shooting baskets and waiting to be called to dinner. My father had been called to a car accident earlier in the day. His car came up the driveway. He had a sullen and worried look upon his face. The accident had been bad. He gingerly stumbled over words and finally got to his point. A friend from high school had been with his father. Another car had hit them head-on. Several people were dead, including my friend's father. The ambulances had been consumed carrying the injured and near dead. My dad had carried my friend's father's body to the hospital. He asked if I would mind cleaning out the back of the station wagon. When I opened the tailgate, there was a large pool of blood soaking into the carpet. The man had suffered a massive head injury, and the telltale pinkish gray matter that forms the brain had splashed about the interior. I was frightened to touch it. I used a pail of

THE FAMILY CAR

water and a sponge. I took my time with each stroke, feeling as though I was erasing a man's life. I slowed my actions to a crawl, wanting to extend to him a few moments more of existence.

Cars and girls in rural communities meant finding lonely roads for a few frantic moments of cuddling. Many times I found myself in intimate situations when the police radio would blare, "Eustice, what are you doing in there." Other times with windows fogged from heated passion, I might hear a tapping of a flashlight on the window and "Eustice, does your old man know what you're doing." The Waseca County deputies seemed to have had an unusual need to know what I was up to and a penchant for finding me.

My dad once gave me a deputy sheriff's badge and the car to go to stock car races in an adjacent county and look for a runaway. Armed with a badge and a picture of the runaway, I was allowed inside without paying. I was sixteen, wearing a muscle shirt and cut-off jeans, and I wasn't challenged. I guess they thought I was working undercover. I returned the car but not the badge. I spent several summers going to races, dances, and concerts and just flashed a badge for admittance. Sometimes I took friends and called them my posse. I was only challenged once.

I was in Minneapolis and I was stopped for speeding. The largest man I had ever seen in my life emerged from the police car. The ground shook with each step he took. He carried a huge nightstick and swung it menacingly with each stride. When he was adjacent to my window, he used the stick to tap on it. He drew a circle in the air with it to signal me to roll my window down and he impatiently tapped on the roof of my car as I struggled to manually get the window down. He asked for my license. I took my billfold from my back pocket, and reaching it out toward him, I flipped the billfold so that the badge immediately caught his eye. He took the billfold and stared at the badge. He stepped back for a moment and peered from behind mirrored sunglasses into my eyes. "So," he drawled, "you're a so-called deputy." He handed me the billfold and walked back to his car. He slowly pulled back into traffic and was gone. I put the wallet back into my pants and checked to make sure it was the only load in my pants.

Rocking Chair Blues

DOUG WAS SIX years old when he would witness his first murder scene. I was twelve when I saw eight-by-twelve glossy black-and-white pictures of the same dead. The pictures had captured the death masks of four individuals, three men and a woman. I recall the woman's picture most vividly. She lay on her right side. She wore a scarf that hid most of her hair and sunglasses that matched the single dark hole in the middle of her forehead.

The deaths were the tragic end of a love story. A young couple broke up, and the jilted boyfriend, unable to express his pain, turned his rage on the object of his love. He killed her two brothers and then shot her. He had surprised them all. The family members died in the farmyard. They all wore their work clothes and died doing their chores. Distraught, the lover/murderer went into the farmhouse. He sat himself in a rocking chair in the front room, pondered his actions, and cried in desolation. He then put the gun in his mouth and joined his lover.

Dad had spent the day at the murder scene. The bodies had been removed, and investigators and the meandering crowds that are attracted by slaughters had all left. Doug does not remember why he went to the scene. He believes someone took him and left him, possibly for Dad to babysit. He recalls being driven into the farmyard. Dad walked out of the house. He gathered Doug up in his arms and carried him into the house. Doug believes Dad was waiting for neighbors to arrive and finish the uncompleted chores. The cows were bellowing loudly, overburdened with milk to be delivered.

As they waited they walked around the farm. Doug remembers snow and mud. In some places blood still glistened in the snow. Doug didn't fully understand the horror of the situation, but he understood Dad's sullenness. My dad's always present great Irish smile had been replaced with firm-lipped sadness.

It was cold and they went into the farmhouse to get warm. Doug recalls the rocker sat separately with a large stain on the floor. The chair seemed lonely. He believes that the unoccupied rocker still moved under its own volition.

Friends Forever

TODD AND HIS friend Kurt cruised the main fairway of the Steele County Fair. Their heads jerked alternately between the food stands and the young girls. Being sixteen years of age had its battles. Mini-donuts and miniskirts had almost equal appeal. The fair was a big deal. It not only marked the end of summer, but it was also a chance to meet young lovelies from a five-county area. The smells and sights of the fair were contagiously delightful.

Todd was checking out a cute brunette standing in line near the Ferris wheel. She had a great smile and everything else. His mind was going to a wonderful place when he felt Kurt's elbow in his side. Wincing he turned to meet his friend's eyes. Kurt's face was drawn with excitement as he jerked his thumb to the left. Todd's eyes followed.

Three curvaceous young girls swung their hips, moving in the direction of the boys. They were all blonde and blue-eyed. They wore similar clothes—tight blouses and very short shorts. One girl stood out. She was prettier than the others. She had a pin-up figure. Todd looked to Kurt. Kurt stared back. Their brains had decoded the same message simultaneously. "It's her!"

Kurt and Todd had been best friends since childhood. They had become inseparable. The girl represented one moment in their short lives that was unforgettable. The event had welded the bond between them. When she approached she noticed their staring. As she passed she may have thought, *How rude*. She wore a metal structure that was allowing a broken neck to heal. That cemented it for Todd and Kurt: it was her.

Five months earlier the boys had been at the Eustice house watching TV and having pizza. The phone rang. Todd's father walked slowly to the phone and used his official sheriff's voice to answer. He hung up and called to the boys. "There's been an accident. Do you want to go?"

Like two large puppies Todd and Kurt were falling over each other to get to the car first. The adrenaline rush of pending danger always won out over Saturday night TV. They threw themselves into the car as it was moving. There wasn't any time to be wasted. The siren was blazing as the car emerged from the driveway. Kurt then heard his father's voice over the police radio. He was driving the ambulance, also rushing to the car accident scene.

The ride to the accident scene itself is a brain-freezing experience. The car becomes a rocket sled.

Bodies are thrown with maximum G force against the doors with each turn and curve. The siren wires the mind for danger. The radio traffic sets nerves on fire. No one talks. Fear is in charge.

Kurt's dad caught up to the sheriff's squad two miles from the accident. Dark was falling and the twin lights and sirens assaulted the peaceful tranquility of a country evening. The official vehicles made a wide, sweeping curve when the boys saw several vehicles parked on the roadside and one vehicle upended in the ditch. Lyle, Kurt's father, pulled up near the overturned vehicle. Todd and Kurt had already exited and were following the sweeping beam of Todd's father's flashlight. A stranger ran up to the boys' fathers and said there were five victims. Four were lying in the ditch; one remained in the car. He was dead.

Someone yelled, "Come on!" The fathers and sons ran toward the living victims.

Crying cannot describe the wailing of those fearing death. It's more like the scream of a wounded animal. It assaults the ears and explodes in the brain. You have to fight all your emotions to force your body to move. Everything is acute. Movement is fast motion. The mind is always overwhelmed.

The boys noticed the injured were all about their age. They followed their fathers' orders as the injured were triaged. "Check the one in the car," someone yelled at the boys. "Make sure he's dead." Todd had the flashlight. He lay on the ground and shone the light into the young man's face. He was lying lifeless in the backseat. Todd first noticed his body was twisted in an unnatural way. The eyes seemed vacant. They stared from nothing into nothingness. Todd said nothing and put his hand up. Kurt pulled him to his feet. They returned to the injured. They both later would say they felt like robots, not thinking or feeling, just listening, reacting to the commands of their fathers.

The men had loaded a young girl onto a backboard. The boys were ordered to carry the young woman to a wheeled gurney waiting on the blacktop road. They gingerly laid her on the stretcher, and Lyle strapped her body down. The boys noticed then that she had a collar around her neck. They were attracted to her beauty washed in blood. They felt stirrings of attraction and pity. She was placed in the ambulance. A second ambulance had arrived, and two injured adolescents were placed in it. Lyle yelled for the boys, "Let's go!" He threw Kurt the keys to the ambulance and jumped in with the injured girl. Todd rode shotgun.

The two ambulances rolled out together. The sirens screamed simultaneously, and the ambulances charged into the night headed toward the best medical care in the world, Rochester, Minnesota. The ride was fast and furious. They pulled into St. Mary's hospital in less than an hour. Hospital staff rushed the ambulances and began assessing the injured immediately. Lyle was helping unload the second ambulance and yelled at the boys, "Stay with the stretcher, I want it back." As they had all evening, they heeded each command.

They ran with the gurney and attendants into the ER. A nurse stopped them at the doors and told them to wait. They pushed past, stating they had been told to stay with the stretcher. They stood at the foot of the stretcher as an intern cut off all the clothes of the young woman in the neck brace. She lay naked before Todd and Kurt. They were reverent at the beauty of the female form. They lost sight of the trauma and felt another overwhelming need, then turned away with a mixture of shame and great awe. They had beheld the glory of a beautiful naked girl.

All this passed through their minds as they now watched her walk past, her head held steady with the pieces of an erector set. They both felt relieved she had lived. They both felt stirrings at the thought of her nakedness. They were alarmed at the mixture of feelings. Todd suggested they get some mini-donuts.

Waving the Flag

IT WAS A long, slow, bone-numbingly slow night. I had hoped for a little action. The Vietnam War was at its ugliest, and the FBI had called the Sheriff's Office and said the courthouse was a target of war protestors. The FBI had obtained information that sometime over the weekend, most likely this night, a group was going to break into the courthouse to destroy draft records. The courthouse had been rigged with a silent alarm system that was monitored at the Sheriff's Office only several hundred feet away. If the doors of the courthouse were opened, a constant buzzing in the alarm at the Sheriff's Office would quit. Silence would shout, "Intruders!" I was dispatching. Only one call had gone out the entire evening and that was for missing cattle. It turned out they weren't even stolen; they had just wandered away. I sat listening to the droning of the alarm. It began to fester in my head like the hum of a large mosquito just out of slapping distance.

At these times my mind just went on hiatus.

Luckily on this journey it stuck on the image of my girlfriend. I was thinking about how stupid I was to be sitting at the radio console when I could have been with her on this steamy night. The thought of her glistening skin dampened by the humid air was starting to overwhelm me when my replacement walked in. We exchanged small talk, and I was thinking he might be lucky enough to be in the middle of some action. I was tired; I was going home to sleep.

I was walking the twelve blocks to my bed. A small breeze mixed with the silent streets to create a Rockwellian moment. I wished the alarm had gone off for no other reason than to have broken the monotony of the evening. I didn't know how I felt about the war any longer. When I had first gone to college, I knew I stood firmly on righteous ground. The first day of classes there had been a large antiwar demonstration on campus. I knew immediately from listening to my father and the news that these "longhairs" were outside agitators trying to stir up some trouble.

The college had a large square in front of the campus church. There were several hundred agitators marching around the square with signs and banners and chanting antiwar slogans. They were being led by a convertible with several people waving large flags with peace signs. The protestors were parading around the square and then following the road down to the football field, where they were planning to interrupt ROTC drills. A large crowd of students watched the procession. As the lead car turned onto the roadway, I instinctively stepped in front of it, forcing it to stop. I then tore a peace flag out of the hands of two protestors and tore it up while shouting at all of the hundreds of protestors, "We don't want your kind here!" I turned and marched back into the crowd thinking my father would be so proud of me. Visions of John Wayne were floating in my head when I was grabbed by the shoulder from behind. I spun around and recognized an English professor standing before me. "What were you thinking of? Are you some kind of troublemaker?" I was puzzled. I believed I had acted as a hero and I was being accused of being the aggressor. I went back to the dorm, where the story of my intervention had already roosted. New acquaintances got in my face all asking the same question, "What the hell is wrong with you?"

I was walking up the driveway, now ambivalent about the war, when my father jumped from the shadows and into his car. He slowed only long enough for me to slide in. "The alarm is off. Someone's in the courthouse."

Yeah! I screamed in my head. *Action!*

The courthouse was surrounded by local deputies and cops. There were two entrances. None seemed to have been tampered with, but we all knew how sly these commie kids were. Half the law enforcement personnel stayed outside to catch the thugs if they attempted to escape. I entered the two-story stone building with half a dozen officers and my father. The plan was helter-skelter. Officers ran throughout the building. Everyone wanted to be the first to contact the enemy within. I ran down a narrow hall that led from the judge's chambers to the courtroom. A large dark figure yelled from the end of the hall, "Stop, or I'll shoot!"

I came to a halt, frozen in my jeans and T-shirt. A flashlight hit my face. "Oh, it's you." He put the light and his gun down. I checked my pants. We were both okay. I ran back out into the great hall. Cops were coming out of all the offices shaking their heads, regretting they had made no contact. I sped up to the second floor, taking three and four steps at a time. At the top of the stairs, a crouching figure demanded, "Stop right there or you're dead!" Another cop and another gun. Apologies were exchanged and I ran down the hall. Only ten minutes gone and I had nearly been shot twice. My better senses returned. I sat down in an office with all its lights on and waited for the all-clear. It wasn't the first time I had had a gun pointed at me, but I was recalling clearly that I was on a hunt for college-age kids in jeans and T-shirts with long hair. I tucked my flowing brown locks under my collar and decided to wait this one out. I still wasn't sure how I felt about the war, but I knew how every one of these officers felt about "dirty hippies."

A false alarm was declared. I was driving home with my father when he spoke to me and to no one in particular. "I'm glad we didn't find any kids."

The Old Man in the Corn

THE OLD MAN lived out near the Morristown cutoff. He farmed on gently rolling hills. His farm was once a showcase, but age and neglect had worn it down like an old dime. The decline had started many years before when his wife had died. She was the glue, and her passing had set him adrift. He knew how to farm and he steadily brought in good crops. He wasn't a good parent, he didn't want to talk, and he couldn't communicate with his adult sons. They had lain around the farm like old coon hounds. They, too, had lost their way. They all sat in the evening, alone in their rooms, looking out at the same stars, but no one in the solitude of the night could see the light. Cataracts were beginning to blur the old man's vision, and booze blinded his boys.

The boys had become enfeebled by the drink in their early thirties. Now in their fifties they avoided each other and had stopped doing even small chores. When the dishes were too encrusted to eat on, they

THE OLD MAN IN THE CORN

were left on the ledge and new ones were bought. Piles of once used china pointed to the steadily building chaos of a once fine home. The largest pile of spent belongings were the pints and quarts of cheap whiskey that grew outside the back door. Both boys liked a little water to cut the bitterness of their addiction, and a ritual had developed. When the last drop of a bottle was poured and mixed with water, each son walked to the door and threw the empty bottle toward the pile of undreamed possibilities.

The old man was finding it harder to bring in each year's crop. His limbs ached of arthritis, and his heart yearned to reunite with his wife. Existence had become depression built upon inconsequence. He brought in help. Grandsons and drifters now toiled where the "sons" refused to tread. The hired hands were usually men one of the sons drank with. They, too, had a love and passion for the hard liquor, but they lacked family and the resources that tired patriarchs could provide. They came to the farm with good intentions. They all started out the first day trying to commit to the farmer's creed of working until the work was done. By the second day they became resentful of the boys and would emulate that which they detested. The farm became a rest home for the wayward drinker. Some drifted away; some died in one of the upstairs bedrooms of malnourishment or ruptured ulcers. They all held on to the last drink.

The old man was running for his life or at least

walking horridly. He stopped to use the phone. My dad answered. "Don, someone's shooting up the house. They're shooting at me. It ain't the kids. One of the hands—one of the hands is crazy with drink, and he's shooting at everyone."

"Get out," my dad said, "and head for the corn." He had taken the call at home. He kissed my mom and yelled into the basement for Doug. "Some trouble—do you want to come with me?" When Doug appeared in the kitchen, Dad said, "Get a gun." Doug went back into the basement and reappeared with a short-barreled twelve-gauge. He was putting shells into his pockets as they walked to the car.

Driving north into trouble, Dad had Doug load his gun in the car. Just to be ready for whatever. Dad radioed the office to ask for backup and to give details. The old man had been angry at the lack of work on the part of this last farmhand. They had argued and the man went upstairs to get his gun. The old man had rushed his boys out the door and shots followed. The old man detoured to make the call. Finishing his conversation with my dad, he ran for the corn.

As Dad's car pulled into the farm driveway, Doug asked Dad if he had heard something. Doug was alert, his finger on the trigger. Dad shrugged. They exited the car and both quickly scanned the yard. There were no bodies in view, and nothing seemed amiss in the tall grass and rusting machines. They both turned to the house when something sounded as if it

THE OLD MAN IN THE CORN

had dropped. The loud bang was followed by absolute silence. Nature seemed to be holding her breath. They ran toward the front door. Dad didn't call out a warning or knock. Gasping for breath he told Doug to knock the door down. Doug smiled to himself as Dad had often used Doug as a battering ram. Doug felt sometimes Dad got a kick out of seeing doors splinter against Doug's boot. Doug reared back and planted his cowboy boot on the door just below the lock. The lock and the top hinge gave way, and the door tilted inward, giving Dad and Doug a clear view of a long, dark hallway.

The main floor of the house was open to view. To the left was the living room. Dead ahead was the kitchen, and to the right was the dining room. Dad went left and Doug right. They met in the kitchen. The trouble had to be upstairs. Dad hesitated at the bottom of the stairs, his .38 short barrel police special pointed toward the ceiling. Doug knew Dad was going to attempt to talk any culprits hidden upstairs to come down. Doug acted quickly. Holding the shotgun across his chest, he charged up the steps. Dad reacted and followed closely behind. At the top of the stairs, they were confronted with a hallway and two closed doors on each side. Dad nodded to Doug to take the doors on the right; Dad took those on the left. Dad reached for the first doorknob and, standing to the side, twisted it, and the door popped open. Nothing. Doug kicked his first door to the floor. The same results, nothing. They both sucked in a second breath and walked to the next set of doors.

Dad stood with his gun to the ready, and Doug booted the next door to the floor. The door hit the floor hard and dust flew up. Doug wasn't sure of what he saw. The mind plays tricks when it is so agitated. The dust settled as Doug's mind confirmed the scene. Just inside the door a single chair sat in the middle of the room. A man sat slumped forward. A gun lay on the floor. The man's arms hung to his side, and his head tilted forward. Blood squirted out in time to his pulse, which was weakening. Dad felt for a pulse. The man wasn't thoroughly dead. He clung to life by a spider's thread. His blood flow slowed as the ambulances siren became louder. Dad and Doug let out long, sour breaths. They tried to make small talk and waited for the stretcher that would take one more lost opportunity out past the corn onto the road for one last long, lonely ride to eternity.

Big Sticks and Cotton Candy

I'M A RURAL kid at heart. I love the county fairs. As a kid, the cotton candy, fast rides, animal barns, and great swirl of commotion and noise were a magnet. At the fair you could get lost in the flow of the crowd. The whirling neon lights and the competing thunderstorms of sound made every kid hyperactive and oppositional.

As a teen the fair opened me to the world of frenzied adolescence. Pretty girls and silly giggles became the draw. Quick peeks into the tent of exotic dancers got the testosterone pumping. The fair became fast rides and pretty girls, mini-donuts and pretty girls, and teen dances and pretty girls. The fair was a wild beast. It exhaled new sensations and wild, exhilarating experiences.

As an older teen I walked the midway dressed in the brown shirt of a Waseca County sheriff's deputy.

PLAYING COPS

I'd swing my wooden baton and feel as powerful as the turbo-charged rides. All thanks to my dad and the county's need to keep down the overtime pay of the real deputies. At fair time in Waseca County, the sheriff's posse was often composed of my brothers and me and a gaggle of senior citizens who spent the majority of their work hours drinking coffee and eating pie at the 4-H pavilion.

We didn't look like much, but we weren't meant to scare anyone either. We represented the passivity and peacefulness of rural Minnesota. Nothing ever happened in Waseca, in Minnesota, in the summer. However, things do change.

In the summer of 1970, a motorcycle gang from the Big City had been using weekend excursions to visit small-town events and terrorize the locals. Jail time and busted heads did not deter their weekend hobby. The bad boys with the big bikes liked to go to the small towns, taunt local law enforcement, start fights, and create general mayhem. I guess it gave them something to talk about the rest of the week, or maybe they earned merit badges, who knows.

With the Waseca County fair scheduled to begin, it was expected we would have our visit. The Sheriff's Office was buzzing with adrenaline, and everyone was jumping and grinding whenever the sound of a Harley sucked the angst out of the middle-age men and straightened them up like wooden pegs.

Trouble was brewing, hell was on wheels, and it

BIG STICKS AND COTTON CANDY

was coming our way. In preparation the posse was called together for a security meeting. The senior members limped in, followed by a group of strutting latent teens. My dad had decided to embrace the numbers in the posse by having me call together the old high school wrestling team. We listened to the report of past disturbances. When we heard how the bikers had dismantled other law enforcement groups, even the wrestlers wanted to sneak out and find other work. I prayed my dad had the cavalry stashed somewhere. I didn't want to be thumped upside the head by some beer-demented motorhead.

I felt a small bit of relief when in place of the usual eighteen-inch nightsticks we were handed oaken clubs, two inches in diameter and four feet long. As I looked around the room, some of the gloom returned as I wasn't sure that with the older men the clubs weren't for battle but more for leaning on. Fear was with us.

Saturday night of the fair was our D-day. The plan was for my friends and me to walk about the carnival as if it was a usual day. We were given radios and if called to alert, we were to run to the main gates of the fair. I knew my friends would have no problem assembling, but I feared that half of the older guys would be claimed by cardiac arrest just having to take a brisk walk. Tension built throughout the evening. Trouble has a way of flipping the stomach faster than the tilt-a-whirl.

PLAYING COPS

I was at the far end of the midway when the air rumbled with the sound of big bikes thundering. The radio came alive and my dad's voice was commanding. The time had come. I ran with the herd to the gates, carrying my club like a samurai sword. My dad stood alone, facing twenty bikers. The men and the bikes growled and hissed at him. He motioned for the posse to surround the bikes. The bike gang shut down their machines and glared at the collection of senior citizens and gangly teens. They seemed amused. Bad news appeared on the corners of their snarling mouths. Snickers and laughter went through the bad boys.

My dad stepped toward the leader. He put out his hand and smiled. Like a carnie barker he welcomed them and encouraged them to "stroll the midway. Have some fun." The gang began to press him, but he held his ground. "While you enjoy yourselves, my deputies here are going to guard your bikes for you. They are beautiful machines, and we don't want anything happening to them." His voice then deepened and became more serious. "Have some fun, but if I hear one bit of commotion, if one fight breaks out, my deputies will destroy your bikes." All the deputies tightened their grips on their big oaken sticks in defiance. You can break bikers' heads and they just stand up for more, but destroy his bike, and you might as well beat his mother, his kids, and his puppy.

The bikers walked down toward the rides and

games. They circled the midway once. They returned mumbling threats, climbed on their bikes, and were gone. Their anger thundered down the road. The posse retreated to the 4-H building and celebrated the great victory with pie a la mode.

Santa and the Sheriff

BEING THE SHERIFF'S kid had its drawbacks but also its rewards. The Christmas of my sixteenth year, my dad was able to land me a job that not only paid hard cash but entailed very little physical labor. Win, win. For the first Christmas in my life I would be flush with cash.

The job was simple. Every evening and Saturday between Thanksgiving and Christmas Eve, I'd borrow the Chamber of Commerce's Santa suit and walk up and down the main street shopping district, visiting businesses and enamoring myself to the shoppers. With the red suit, poly white beard, and a newly acquired deeper adolescent voice, I patrolled the holiday streets with a vengeance. I captured the smiles of parents as I teased their children with gentle laughs and lots of free candy. Big plus, teenage girls thought that a giant red elf was flirtatious fun.

I was paid by the hour, but the big money came on Christmas Eve, when I was allowed to use the suit

SANTA AND THE SHERIFF

at private parties. People paid handsomely for a live Santa to stuff their children's stockings.

I had a half-dozen appearances to make in a short couple of hours. I not only needed a fast sleigh but a reliable driver. It wouldn't work for Santa to be seen driving himself around in a 1964 Chevy Biscayne station wagon.

My dad agreed to be my chauffeur. He was always on call, so we used his unmarked sheriff's car. My sleigh wasn't red, but it did come with attachable magnetic red lights and a siren.

I arrived at my first job excited and in a hurry. My dad dropped me off and agreed to circle the block until I reemerged. As arranged, I quietly knocked and was let in the back door. My host informed me that the children were in the basement and were being entertained by other adults. The whole family was gathered around the fireplace singing carols and excitedly awaiting my arrival. I loaded my bag with gifts and nodded to my host that I was ready. She signaled down the steps and "Here Comes Santa Claus" rang out from the basement. On cue, I burst down the stairs, my bells jingling, and my feet pounding the steps. I rushed into the room, bursting with exuberance. I let out my heartiest HO, HO, HO!

Four of the five fearful toddlers desperately grabbed for their parents. The fifth disappeared behind a chair. Older children followed suit. An infant wailed an alarm. The first lesson I learned that night was not all children will receive a six-foot, two-hundred-pound red elf with a face full of fur as friendly. After order was restored and gifts handed out, I apologized, collected my pay, and caught my circling ride.

Having learned from that experience, I approached the next group of children more cautiously. I smiled broadly and laughed gently. The children were enthralled; the lady of the house, embraced with cheer and bourbon, was ecstatic. She came out of nowhere, and her ruby lips pummeled Santa's lips and cheeks. The second lesson I learned that night was to always keep the husband between Santa and well-intentioned but well-lubricated middle-class housewives.

On the way to my next appointment, I was wiping off the lipstick and my dad's police radio crackled to life. My schedule went on hold as we responded to a call of a car in the ditch on the edge of town.

It was a beautiful Christmas Eve evening. The snow was fresh and piled waist high. It was hard and sparkled and crunched as you walked on it. New flakes were falling as we approached the stalled vehicle. The back window of the car was filled with brightly wrapped gifts. The driver was alone and didn't respond to my dad's voice. He approached the car and leaned into the driver's window for what seemed an eternal conversation, then took his hanky out of his pocket and handed it to the driver. He stood erect, turned to me, and motioned for me to approach. As I walked to the vehicle, a woman slowly exited. My father took her arm and stabilized her. He then gently took her shoulders and faced her in my direction. "Here's Santa," he reassured. "Everything will be all right now." The woman's blackened eyes erupted with a torrent of tears. She buried her face into my pillowed stomach and sobbed until I shook like a bowl full of jelly.

My dad backed the woman's car out of the ditch. The woman got into the passenger side, and my dad signaled me to follow them while he drove the gift-laden vehicle. The tears in my beard glistened as headlights and streetlights danced across it.

We reached the woman's home, and I pulled into the driveway. Three pairs of little eyes peeked out from drawn curtains. They ran to the door as Santa and the sheriff escorted their mother. I entertained the frightened children. We shared broken cookies and spilled milk. The woman went to her car and returned her arms laden with gifts. I gave each of the children a final hug and whispered into each ear a quiet "Merry Christmas."

Just as quietly I glided into the kitchen and helped my dad lift her assailant by the arms and legs. Her husband, the father of the children, was too drunk to walk. We carried him out to the car. The snow was beginning to fall harder, creating a winter wonderland. The wind blew cold, but my tears flowed warm.

All in the Family

I HAD SPENT the day in a thirty-foot-deep ditch laying sewer pipe to the new high school. A cool shower had drenched my body clean of the cement particles and dark clay. It had revitalized my tired muscles, and I was looking forward to the start of the weekend and a first date with a particular dark-haired beauty. I put on a shirt purchased just for the special evening, slapped on some cologne, and headed out the door.

I met my dad just coming home. "Where you off to?" he asked.

"Got a date," I shouted over my shoulder as I climbed into the car.

The evening couldn't have been planned any better. She was as spirited and delightful as she was beautiful. We went out of town and caught a movie. We were relaxed and without pretensions in each other's presence. The evening was veering toward the memorable, to the top of the all-time great dates chart.

We returned to Waseca and cruised the main drag

to see who else was out on such a wondrous night. The street was alive, and each car we met was full of friends waving and honking their horns. Word was passed from car to car that a big kegger was being held south of town. I didn't drink as I didn't want to embarrass my father, the sheriff. But hey, everyone was going to be there, and sitting at a large campfire with my arm around my date seemed a dream. I parked my car and we climbed into another vehicle with friends and joined the long parade of vehicles moving toward the great party.

Ten miles south of town, the parade slowed and the great chain of cars pulled into the yard of an abandoned farmstead. Three kegs stood uncorked, oozing their juice into colorful plastic cups. A large fire burned at the back of the skeletal farm home. Dark was descending. My date and I snaked our way through the crowd, and I put my coat on the ground for her to sit. We leaned back against a fallen tree and took in the circus atmosphere. The early arrivals stoked on beer and ditch weed were chattering insanely. A stereo system had been rigged and everyone was swaying and jumping to the sounds of the Doors. A great evening was quickly turning into a spectacular night.

I stretched my legs out toward the fire, put my arm around my date, and pulled her closer. I briefly kissed her high cheekbone, and she pushed up against me. I was burning hotter than the fire's embers.

I was laughing at someone's inane comment and

moving toward my next kiss, which I intended to plant on the prettiest of rosy red lips, when a body hurdled over my head, sidestepped the fire, and was running for the corn. The sprinter's last words as he entered the field were "Eustice, your old man is here!" One hundred bodies were now in full flight. The party was being raided by the Waseca County Sheriff's Department, and my dad was at the lead.

I grabbed my date's hand and ran for the cover of the crops. It was chaos multiplied seven hundredfold. I ran with my date at my side till we were both out of breath. We were confronted with the logistics of being ten miles from town and no transportation. We crept out of the corn and hid at the bottom of the ditch. Time passed slowly and I wasn't quite sure of the next move, when cars started to emerge from the party grounds. I kneeled toward the top of the ditch. I was going to flag down a ride. The first car approached and I started to stand when the car's dome light came on, and I saw my father sitting in the front passenger seat. I fell to the ground hoping to God he hadn't seen me.

Ten miles walking in the dark is a bitch. Four hours later I was giving my date a good night kiss and then I sprinted for home. I ran through the shadows and passed the Sheriff's Office. A dozen cars were parked on the street, including my dad's. I was confident I would beat him home.

I jumped into bed and had barely slowed my

ALL IN THE FAMILY

heart and breath to a restful place when I heard my father's car pull into the driveway. I sensed him standing over me. I feigned sleep. He stood quietly judging my true condition. He left and as his footsteps cleared the stairs, I breathed out a huge sigh of relief and fell asleep believing I had beaten the odds.

I slept soundly and guilt-free. The phone rang about 9 a.m., and no one was answering, so I crawled out of bed and picked up the receiver. It was my mom. "You need to come up to the office."

Before I could get the "why" out, my dad was on the phone. "Where were you last night?"

"On a date."

"What did you do?"

"We saw a movie?"

"I spent the night with most of your friends. You weren't out at a party?"

I was going to lie, but I hesitated and before I could confess, he injected, "Come up to the office, NOW!"

I walked into the sheriff's jail, and my mom was in the front office. She gave that look, the one that says in a motherly fashion, "Your ass is grass."

I walked past and stood in front of my father's desk. "I gave all your friends tickets last night for underage consumption." He pulled one more ticket from the book and handed it to me.

"I wasn't drinking," I pled.

"But you were there. That's going to cost you fifty bucks."

I returned to the outer office and my smirking mother. She had a receipt book open and was ready to take my fine money.

"I don't have any money, Mom."

"Well, your father said you are not to leave here without paying." So much for family trust, I thought.

With my back against the wall, I called my brother Doug, and he brought me my bail money.

Arrested by my dad, booked by my mother, bailed out by my brother. Families don't get any closer than that.

Other Stories That I Tell

A Late Summer Samaritan

I DIDN'T SEE him until I'd committed myself to the freeway off-ramp. From the corner of my eye, I had noticed the sign and his long, unkempt hair. I shot a quick look in his direction; he had the mad eyes of Rasputin and a beard that could have housed all the wrens in the county.

My ten-year-old son called for me to read the sign. In large unsteady print it said, "Need ride anywhere, HOMELESS." Colin called out, "Dad, his shirt is all ripped." It was late fall and the afternoon sun was low. He had to be chilled. I felt some guilt and I tried to avoid looking into the man's eyes. I glanced at my wife and then at the oncoming traffic. I rolled through the stop sign so not to give the homeless stranger any opportunity to connect. I drove to a gas station and kept my back turned to the stranger. I was thinking that if I didn't see him, he couldn't see me and then there should be no expectations.

I paid for the gas and walking to the car I looked. He remained a lonely sentinel at his post. In the car my wife leaned toward me and whispered, "Colin's sad. He thinks we should do something for that man." I can't say that my compassion kicked in. It could have been guilt. I wanted my son's respect, and what was a few dollars? I pulled into the Golden Arches and got one large value meal to go. I was ready for the exchange. Hand the stranger a meal and resolve any guilt.

Heading to the down ramp I stopped and motioned the charity victim over. He sat on the ground seemingly oblivious to my call. He was making it hard for me to demonstrate my Christian compassion. He was making me angry. I stopped the car and walked toward him. His first reaction was a startled response. The smell of the greasy fries lowered his defenses. His head came up and he had a large toothless grin. "Thanks, man." I looked away, avoiding the personal. He took the bag while I stared at my feet. "Wow, man, you shouldn't have." He sounded truly appreciative. "Which way you traveling?" he asked.

Not to be trapped I shot back, "Which way you going?"

I was looking into space, and his answer came from the same direction. "I'm a citizen of Wisconsin, Minnesota, and the US of A and the world. I'm a son of this universe. I can go anywhere I please and anywhere you'd like to take me."

My wife looked a little nervous as I helped our new interplanetary traveler into our earth-bound car. I introduced him to my family. "Hi, I'm Chris," he said happily. Avoiding both his and my wife's stares, I said, "Chris is traveling and asked to ride with us for a short distance." My wife's elbow told me a short distance could be an eternity.

With every click of the odometer, I checked my guest out in the rearview mirror by pretending to be watching traffic. His eyes darted about and when they targeted me, I would quickly look away. I was just giving him a ride. I didn't need to know anything more about him than his destination.

Clumsily making conversation, I called his attention to the late afternoon sun, which lay lazily among purple and pink clouds. "Did you know they have lasers?" he responded. "They can turn them against the earth anytime they wish. I'm not sure what stops them."

I glanced to the mirror. No traffic, no sharp objects in sight. His eyes looked toward mine in the mirror. I changed its angle. I ignored his desire for human interaction and turned on the radio. My wife was feeling more gracious and she started some chitchat. "Where are you from?" he asked her.

"Up north," I offered.

"Originally," he asked.

"Waseca, southern Minnesota," I answered.

Nothing more was said for thirty minutes. I'd check the mirror for traffic, meet his eyes, and quickly turn away.

"Pull over here, this is fine," he said matter-of-factly.

Relieved, I took the opportunity to end this relationship. I helped him with his gear. Shook his hand and wished him well. He started up the ditch and walked toward a country road. I assumed he was looking for a culvert for the night. He stopped after a few feet and turned to me, puzzled. He yelled over the roar of passing cars, "Waseca…do you remember Herter's and the Izzards?!"

Herter's was a twenty-year-old memory. A store of fabled sporting goods created in my hometown. Izzards was a code for midnight rendezvous when I was a teenager. We snuck out of our homes and met at designated spots to taunt the local cops and break everyone's summer monotony. "Chris!" I yelled. "Chris!" He was gone. Had he been a childhood friend? Was he the cousin of a friend visiting one summer? Or maybe a summer visitor who gotten caught up in an adolescent ritual. Did I know him then? Had we run from the cops together on some hot summer night? Maybe we had hidden in the same bushes, breathlessly waiting for the heavy footsteps to pass.

I called after him. I wanted to strengthen those tentative bonds. He didn't hear me. He continued his journey to everywhere and nowhere. He never looked back. Our eyes never met. We never connected.

Winter's Discourse

"THE PROBLEM ISN'T you or I; it's the system." The day was gray with one continuous dark cloud along the horizon and the waters of Superior icy black. "I'm a man of the water. I was born in water and I've lived next to this great body of water my entire life." These words came from Tom, directed to me without even an introduction. I was standing at the bar rail trying to order a Jameson. "Where are you from?"

"I'm from Hibbing."

"I was just up there, with a friend on business. He was talking to some folks from...it started with an ir or ri, doesn't matter. I was disoriented. I was away from the water. I get inland and I lose my way. I couldn't get awkward, outside of myself. How does anyone live away from water?"

I assumed now that he was directing his conversation toward me. Even without my Jameson in hand, I replied, "We've got holes. The biggest holes in the ground in the world are on the Range, and we've got water in

... He didn't call me an idjit. He might have, but he was contemplating much larger equations.

"You see those waters out there?" It was rhetorical. "I wake up to the waves, and they talk to me before I fall to sleep. I don't know how to live away from the water."

I picked up my glass, raised it toward Tom while holding out my right hand. "I'm..." and I was lost in the draping of a great coat and scarf. She had jumped on my back but squirmed around so we were face-to-face.

"Hi, Tony."

"I'm not Tony. My name's Gary."

"Good to see you again." Then she climbed down and scampered to the end of the bar with a group of young men.

I tipped my drink to Tom and retreated to a table in the back. Anne was waiting. I told her this was quite a friendly group. We chatted pleasantly and then I noticed my Jameson had evaporated, so back to the rail. I stood at the bar with Tom to my right. He was lost in the crashing of the big waves outside the window. I held my glass high, catching the eye of the bartender, who acknowledged me with a nod.

"Hi, I'm John." I twirled left. I held out my hand, "Hi, I'm..." and a young man at the end of the bar next to the woman I had worn as drapery tipped his glass and yelled across the bar, "Hey, Gary." I smiled and waved to the stranger.

John took my hand. "Hi, Gary. You see those waters? I came up here from Green Bay to find my balance. I've been remade. Where are you from?"

"Hibbing."

"Never been there."

"Giant holes in the ground, John. It's iron country."

"Yes, mining. That's about taking." He put his fist out and pulled it back into his chest with a thump. "There's no balance there. What happened to us? What happens when we just take? There's no balance."

I picked up my Jameson and with a small salute, I took a sip. "Dylan was born there. That's got to create some balance."

"Yes, Dylan," John pondered. "There is some balance there."

John spoke in hushed tones with an intonation that reminded me of the way Native Americans speak.

"You native, John?"

"No, I'm German, from a long line of Germans. Are you native, Gary? You look native."

"No, I'm Irish."

"You're a damned big Irish. You're the biggest Irishman I've ever met. What happened to my people, Gary? They lost their balance. Those Nazis, they were just people. No different than you or me. They lost their balance. They did horrible things. They hurt so many. They allowed a little insane man to lead them into terrible atrocities. They had no balance. They forgot to think for themselves. Look at our economy.

There's no balance with our leaders. No balance with the people. We've become takers. No one gives back. There is no balance. I'm regaining my balance. I've been remade."

"How were you remade, John?"

"It's not important. It's not about God. It doesn't matter what I believe or what you believe. You have to find balance. My people were farmers. My dad had a big dairy. That's of the earth. There's balance in that. My father was hard and he worked us hard, but there was balance. What did your dad do?"

"He was a sheriff."

"That's the work of being a balancer. There are so many troubled people. Hurt people. Your dad brought them balance. He balanced out the physically bad and evil."

"I'll tell you a story of balance, John. My father's ancestors were sheriffs in Ireland for many generations. That was just what the family did. My mother's ancestors lived in a nearby county, and for many generations they were sheriffs. Then in the 1850s, my father's great-grandfather came across the ocean to New York and crossed the country to southern Minnesota. My mom's family crossed to Canada and traveled to Missouri before arriving in Minnesota. My mom and dad met and they dated only each other. They married and my father became the sheriff without any knowledge of his history. How's that for balance."

"That's amazing. That's balance. Did you create that balance? I didn't create that balance. How did that balance get there? We take and create imbalance. Who corrects things, who puts things back in balance? I've been remade. I now see the imbalances. I want to correct them. We need to give back."

I twirled the ice in my Jameson and watched the whirlpool in my glass.

"What do you do, Gary?"

I laughed as I always do when asked this question. "I'm a psychologist."

"Then you're a balancer too! You see all the harm and pain people do to each other, and you helped those lost in that pain. You put the mental and emotional balance back into their lives."

"Well, thank you, John. I never thought of it that way."

"You are a balancer; your father was a balancer. That's balance! There is great balance in this world."

My wife waved to me that it was time to go. I returned to the bar later that evening. Neither Tom nor John were present. The room had been taken over by young people, embracing the loud music and the football game on five different screens. They seemed unaware of the water, and balance was becoming a question.

Wounded Flower

SHE LAY IN the grass and mud, a wounded flower. There wasn't a body part that didn't hurt more than any other. She was collage of bruises. Her head pulsated like an anvil being slammed by the hammer of Thor. Disturbing thoughts of a hundred dark colors ricocheted inside her skull. She closed her eyes and waited for a cold death. "Stupid bitch" could have been her last thought, but she spat it out with blood and a couple of teeth. "I'm not going to let some dead-ass fuck shit kill me." She reached for her clothing. She thrust about in the dark. "He stole them, the little cunt!" She was lying on top of her shredded bra. She grasped it and tried to roll over. Pain pushed her face into the dirt again. She lay quietly fighting for breath. She rolled to her back and gazed at the brilliant sky. She looked to one great star. She fixed her sight on it and reached out her swollen hands. She grabbed at the beautiful heavenly body and pulled herself erect. Her knees buckled but she righted herself. *Fuck him*, she thought.

Forty-five minutes earlier she had been making a deal. She had some extra pot to sell. He was buying. She had noticed him drinking heavily at the party. He was the only one drinking more than she. She approached him. He said he felt uncomfortable making the buy where others might see it go down. *Chickenshit*, she thought to herself. Everyone at the party was a known stoner. She needed the money, so she blew off her caution and went out to his car. Inside the vehicle he said he still didn't feel comfortable. "Cops could drive by."

She pulled on the door handle to leave but then had second thoughts. "All right, head up this street two blocks, hang a left, and we'll be on an old mining road. No cops, no streetlights. Will you feel safe then?"

He pulled slowly away. He was quiet. He got to the mining road and kept driving. "You can stop anywhere now, friend," she said.

"A little farther."

She tiredly slouched back into the seat and lit a doobie. "Want some?"

"Thanks."

"Don't fuckin' mention it. It's all part of the deal," she squealed. She found the world hilarious whenever she toked.

He pulled over into a large field. There was enough starlight to see it was a place kids came to party. Fire rings and beer cans were the field's major features. She got out and took an extra-large toke. He came around the car. He was looking at his shoes all nervous like. She was going to say something lightly teasing when his left hand hit her right temple and she fell to the ground. He began stomping her with heavy boots. She cried and wailed to the rhythm of each kick. He kept time to the screams with a steady pulse of pounding shoe wear, and they created a small symphony. She was nearly unconscious, and he dragged her by her feet farther into the field. He stopped near a large rock, climbed up on it, and jumped down onto her head with his knee. He pulled her to her feet and began slapping her face. The blows alternately knocked her unconscious and then would revive her. The pain shook to her knees, and she thought dying was a pretty good deal. She would start to fall, and he'd knock her upright with his fists. He backed away. She stood swaying in the wind. Her bloody eyes did not allow her to see the big windup. His fist blasted into her stomach, knocking the wind from her lungs. It lifted her off her feet and slammed her backward three feet. She landed on her stomach, twisting in midair. He began stomping her back, then rolled her over like cord wood. He put his knee on her neck and pulled her blouse up. He cut the bra off. She was too weak to cry or resist. He rolled her onto her back and took her clothes. The sharp coldness of the hard ground awakened her. *No, not again*, she thought, as he did what he wanted.

WOUNDED FLOWER

When he had exhausted his entire sexual prowess, he put his hands around her throat and began to squeeze. She knew she was going to die. She recovered a memory, a trick she had seen in a movie. The heroine had feigned dying, and the bad man, fooled, walked away. She held her breath and went limp. Her lungs burned. She fought breathing to live. She fought crying for her mother. She fought dying. He got up, gathered her clothes, and went to the car.

Hours or minutes later, she stumbled to her feet. She didn't notice the car at first. She stood, stunned to be alive. If death could relieve the pain, she would now welcome it. But she was a fighter. She had fought her father. She had fought her brother and how many of his asshole friends. She heard the noise of the engine first. She turned toward the growl of the car and saw it was still parked. A little red bud of light in the driver's seat pinpointed her assailant. She was furious. Who the fuck was he to kill her and then take her dope?

He felt amazingly calm. He had found this feeling by accident several years and many girls ago. Now he sought it out as often as he could. Without the rough sex his mind was a tumult of anger and vengeance. He had difficulty concentrating and sleeping. But the girls made all the difference, and he felt no remorse. He felt a sweet silence. He sat quietly experiencing a remarkable moment of calmness. As he blew out some smoke, he felt at ease, a simple peacefulness. His mind was dulled, his nerves settled.

He closed his eyes and started to dream. Wind hit his face, and a cold harshness blew through the passenger door.

"YOU FUCKER, you're taking me to the hospital." She grabbed the joint from his fingers and took a large drag, bogarting it. She exhaled a barrage of condemning salutations all begun with "mother" or "shit." "You get this shit heap moving and get me to the hospital now," she demanded.

Stunned at the bleeding, screaming banshee beside him, he turned the car and headed back into town. He stumbled over words as he tried to apologize. He pleaded that she not tell. He was a felon. He would be back in prison. She couldn't do that to anyone, could she? He felt like crying. He was panicked. She became stone quiet in her pain. She concentrated on her breathing. She tried to slow it down so her ribs did not shriek with stabbing pain. She mumbled, "You fucking baby! Get me to the hospital and I won't say anything." She then went into a seething rant about his parenthood, manhood, sexual skills, and general lame-ass ways.

He let her off at a block from the hospital. The ER entrance was half a block away. He was scared. She was barely out of the car and he sped off. His taillights became red pinpoints in the blackness of the town's streets. She stood naked, caked in blood, smeared in mud and grass. She held her bra in her left hand. Each step was a mountain to climb. She moved trancelike, a zombie walk, half falling forward with each step. She reached the driveway to the ER and reassured herself she was going to live. She pushed herself uphill. A cop stood in the lobby behind great panes of glass. He stood gazing as she approached with his mouth agape and a dopey look in his eyes. She got to the doors and hit the automatic opener. The cop was frozen; he slowly lifted an arm, and a single digit pointed to the ER doors. She handed him her bra, thinking it was evidence, and staggered into the ER.

I saw her two days later in my office. Her face was swollen and her eyes were blackened. She walked carefully, gingerly. Each step eked a small wince of pain from her lips. She sat down exhausted. "Every shrink I've ever seen gives me a different diagnosis, but they all think I'm crazy. What do you think?"

"You're hurt."

"No shit, Sherlock."

"I'm sorry this happened to you."

"Glad you noticed."

We were off to a good start.

Between Hope and a Hard Place

SOMETIMES LIFE DEALS the cards from the bottom, and hopelessness can seep in before the first hand is even played. Macy was thirty-eight when she decided to straighten the deck and ask for help. Up till then her life had been a confusing maze of trauma and pain blurred by drugs and alcohol.

Macy came into the world looking for encouragement and needing love and nurturance. When she looked into her mother's eyes, nothing reflected. Great empty sockets of depression and alcoholism pushed Macy away. Macy's mother had a trick of disappearing for days at a time. Her greatest trick was once to never return. Macy's dad drank away his rejection. He couldn't give his full attention to Macy, so he gave it to alcohol. Macy sat in her own excrement until her mouth opened to cry and only the dust of discouragement spewed forth. The state took her away from her father. Paternal neglect and abuse cannot be tolerated. Macy was an infant when her aunt rescued her. She was two when her aunt died.

When no relative wants you, the game of foster care is played. It's a lot like Russian roulette. The odds are you're going to get hurt. She was in many placements. She was never secure. She was pushed from placement to placement and labeled a malcontented child. At age four she was placed in foster care at the home of a local cop. He and his wife had a reputation for correcting the behavior of the most grievous young children. By age eight she was the constant bed companion of the man of the house. Macy was so good that the man introduced his sixteen-year-old son to her in ways only men know how to make introductions. The mother of the house feigned ignorance but made sure she beat the child weekly. So a cycle was established. Sexual assault, run away, get beaten. Life is not only a circus; it's a merry-go-round of pain and humiliation for "bad" children.

You can run but you can't hide. Drugs sure numb the soul. Macy drank and smoked dope daily. It let the caged bird twitter. At sixteen she ran away for the last time. Life became a parade of abusive men. She learned to dance to entertain men. She drank when she danced so she didn't have to feel the pain of those stupid eyes that wanted to rape her but were owned by slovenly drunk dicks who couldn't put the beer down long enough to complete any act, be it human or otherwise. The rapes had numbed her to pain; the beatings reawakened the shame.

The man she thought was "it" forced her into prostitution before she was twenty-one. His beatings caused concussions. The concussions created brain damage. Memories became hard to hold except for the ones she wanted to release. When the fog of drugs wasn't enough to keep the monsters of dreams and reality away, she learned to "just" leave. She would sense herself circling around the ceiling while watching that little bitch take what she deserved. She thought it was cool, and was later told it was dissociation.

At age thirty-seven, Macy had a revelation. It wasn't God or the saints. It wasn't wise words written. She was being walked at night from a car in the Nevada desert to her death. Tired of beating her, her new pimp thought he'd put an end to this nuisance. Somewhere on that dark path she told herself that she'd had enough. She turned on her would-be murderer and threatened to kick his ass if he wasn't brave enough to put one between her eyes right then and there. She picked up a rock and beat herself on the head, howling like an injured coyote. She wailed with the pain of a thousand assaults. The assailant was shook from his moorings by this madwoman of the night who railed at the moon and stars, damning all beneath. He ran like a coward.

She fell to the ground. She lay still…minutes, hours, maybe days. She then awakened to the fact she was alive. She never had any luck. She hit the road. Homeless and penniless she found her way back to the north woods of Minnesota. She found someone who listened to the pain without judging. She took some meds that didn't just blot out the horizon. She found shelter. She found community. She found hope.

Christmas Confessions

WHEN I WAS a child, my family lived across the driveway from my maternal grandparents. The driveway became a two-way street during the holidays. Christmas Eve we would go to my grandparents for dinner. We would receive a call at dark that Santa had arrived and left hurriedly. When we entered the back door, the aroma of ham and the traditional fixings of Christmas engulfed the house. The presents would be placed under the silver aluminum Christmas tree, and a color wheel spun, casting Christmas color upon the foil needles. The house lights were dimmed for extra effect. Grandpa had a cardboard chimney made to look like red brick. It had a red cellophane flame. It all looked real on such a mythic night.

Dinner was eaten in orderly fashion, as my grandmother was very proper. Dessert had to wait until we had mercifully opened our presents. Grandpa would sit in his chair. Grandmother and my parents found chairs lined against the wall. Grandpa would direct activity, and Doug, the oldest, would play Santa's helper. He would pick up a present as directed by Grandpa and then slowly deliver it to an anxious child. We would become so involved in the process, we failed to see that my father would sneak out. Between socks, fruit, and one special present each, he would magically disappear.

When all the gifts were opened and everyone was involved in show and tell, my dad, never missed, would suddenly appear again. He would go to a window and exclaim, "There goes Santa, and he's leaving our home." It was a race next door and a second helping of Christmas cheer.

By late grade school, I had six siblings. Christmas was nice but presents were more expensive and dreams carried more expectations. It was hard for my parents to fulfill the Christmas wishes. Doug took over. He and I had paper routes and both delivered the morning editions. My route took me downtown. I would stop at the bakery at 6 a.m. and get fresh pastries, still warm. They'd steam on winter mornings. My path would always cross the milk man. I'd stop his truck and get a quart of chocolate milk. Doug was all business. He'd put every dime he earned into a savings account held by the newspaper company. What I didn't spend on my morning ritual, comic books, and Saturday matinees I put aside. It was meager compared to Doug's stash.

At Christmas our customers were often very generous and would give us a large tip or present of money.

We did okay at this happy time of year. Customers would ply us with candy, cookies, and hard, cold cash. We'd often make an extra twenty dollars at Christmastime.

Doug had a routine. Late Christmas Eve afternoon, Doug would find me, and we'd be off to do our Christmas shopping. Doug had several hundred dollars, which was a lot back then. He'd buy multiple presents for everyone. I'd throw in a few chocolate-stained dollars for the little extras. Doug was a whirlwind. He knew what everyone wanted, and we hurried from store to store. He would buy all the expensive presents my parents couldn't afford for my siblings. He made Christmas. We'd sneak the presents into our basement bedroom and wrap them silently. Doug would sign all the gifts from Santa. Doug's presents and the squeal of delight as they were opened was Christmas. Doug was Santa.

During our shopping trip I'd always buy Doug a new shirt in the most recent fashion. He'd open his present, check the size, and throw it to me. Somehow it always was a perfect fit for me.

Christmas Eve Messiahs

IT WAS THE day before Christmas, and I had to work until noon. I had only three appointments. The first person of the day rolled into my office, literally. Her tears erupted from emotional scars, and the pain propelled her along on misaligned hips. Each step was excruciating. She rolled her body to put less weight on the fragile joints. She sighed sitting down. It was a deep, life-supporting, death-wishing sigh. She was tired now. She had been fighting the depression for endless months. Her story was so familiar. Her father physically abused her as a child. A family friend sexually abused her. She was raped as an adult. She tried marriage once, and he was a beast. She left him after two years of torture and two beautiful children. She went to school to learn a trade to support her children and bought them a home. The children grew up to be average middle-class kids with soccer and music recitals. She met all their needs. When they left home and started their families, then she collapsed.

Her body had betrayed her at an early age, but she persevered, too frightened to slow down. She knew from the quiet times in her life that if she let her guard down, angry, hurtful thoughts worked their way from the darkest corners of her mind and made her tremble. She pushed her broken body past its limits to keep the secrets of her past from seeping into conscious life. With her body broken, she lost her business, her home, and her confidence.

Now she faced me and cried tears for the physical pain she lived with daily, tears for the shame of losing her middle-class identity, tears for the shame of needing to accept public support, and tears for an uncertain and fearful future. She shed no tears, however, for the little girl robbed of her childhood. No tears were shared for the little girl beaten. She held back tears for the young woman ravaged. She would not dare open those floodgates. She kept her focus forward, and dared not look back. But unspeakable truths from the past have a way of coming into the light. She needed to embrace that part of her, but she refused and her depression mounted.

I offered solace and options. I suggested she face the demons that pursued her. She feared the trip alone. "I might go to a support group," she offered.

"Yes, you might, and I'm sure you would help the others considerably. But what about you?"

"What about me?"

"Who will help you?"

There was a long silence. A great struggle was ensuing. "I will help me."

We made the appropriate referrals. "Merry Christmas," she said as she left.

He came in with a face reddened with years of whiskey abuse. He was late. "I had to see my brother. He's in detox. The doctor said he'd be dead by Valentine's Day if he does not stop drinking. I went to say goodbye. I went to say goodbye." He shook with anxiety. He wrapped his arms around himself to stop the tremors.

"My wife died in February this past year. She was the only one that has ever loved me. I miss her. I've drank daily for thirty years. She always wanted me to stop. When she died I couldn't stop drinking, but I stopped living. I've been on a ten-month binge. I just stopped trying. Now I'm homeless. I let everything go." He sucked in a big gulp of air. He wrapped his arms around his legs to stop the limbs from shaking. Then a big smile came over his face. "I haven't had a drink for three days. "

"Merry Christmas," I said.

My last client of the day walked in smiling. His nose was pushed against the left side of his face and wrapped around his cheek. A ragged scar ran from his forehead to his chin. "Bipolar, I'm bipolar. I need to get back on medication. I haven't had my meds in three months. I can feel a depression starting. I need meds."

"How depressed do you get?"

He opened his shirt and showed me a large angry red badge of flesh over his heart. "This depressed. This chest scar is a twenty-two. If you really want to die, don't shoot yourself in the heart with a twenty-two. There's no guarantee." He pointed at his face. "Shotgun, can't do anything right. I sneezed as I pulled the trigger."

I made some calls and arrangements so he could get refills of his psych meds. He was pleased. "Thanks, partner," he said as he left.

"No problem."

He peeked back in. "Have a Merry Christmas," he said.

"You too!"

Mental Health Days

DAYS GET STRENUOUS even though I don't really do anything that exerts any physical energy. Even so, I occasionally just take a day off. Everyone needs mental health days. Right? I decided a road trip was needed. I was seventy miles into my trip to nowhere when my phone rang. Challenge, do I answer it? I let it go to voicemail. I was fidgeting with the radio, trying to get a clearer signal to NPR, and the phone rang a second time. "Hell. Gary speaking." I recognized the voice of my secretary, but the message kept breaking up. "I'm near a black spruce swamp. There's a hill ahead, hang on. Okay, I can hear you now. What's up?"

Her voice had an edge and she spoke rapidly. "Staci Jackson's husband has kidnapped her and is holding her at gunpoint. He's willing to talk to you. Where are you?"

"Who's doing what?"

"Staci Jackson's husband kidnapped her this morning and is threatening to kill her, but she said he will come in and talk to you."

Staci had married her high school sweetheart because she was afraid not to. He was what we call on the Range a Jack Pine Savage. He liked physical work, but for the most part was allergic to it. He hated everyone except his mom and dad. He drank too much. He fought a lot, especially when he drank. Women were to be in the house, and children were to stay out of the way. Women made good house servants and were useful sex slaves, but don't allow them an education.

He felt Staci wasn't sexually stimulating after fifteen years of marriage, so he turned to their teenage daughters. Staci had many reasons to walk out on him. She never could do it just for herself. She found the courage to protect her daughters. She got a restraining order, cooperated with the police, and filed for divorce.

His reaction was from the gut. "I'll kill the bitch!" He tried the old cons first. Love letters and pleading phone calls of apology. Staci reacted strangely. She didn't buy into it. She called the police again and he was arrested for violating his restraining order. "The bitch must die." He was humiliated. He'd never let a stray dog bite him, much less a woman. HIS woman was going to show respect and die.

"Where are they now," I asked.

"They're driving around, but they will meet you at the office."

"I'll be there in one hour. Will she be safe?"

"She thinks so."

Winter, icy roads, and an hour's drive back. I turned around and headed for home. I arrived within forty minutes. My wife had gone along for the ride and was as pale as the snow. I jumped out of the car as it rolled to a stop. "I'll find my own way home, dear."

My office is in a renovated school. I entered at a run. An old voice in my head reminded me you don't run in the school halls. I slowed to a trot and was met by staff. "They're in the testing room."

"Does he have a gun?"

"We didn't see any. Staci looks awful. What's happening?"

"I'll let you know."

My pace quickened and my stomach churned. It wasn't unlike being called to the principal's office.

I play many different roles in my life. I've developed a routine for the changing of roles. I stop at the door, take a deep breath, and put on the mask of empathy, the counselor's look, and I say to myself as the door opens, "It's showtime."

They were sitting at the end of a long table. I tried to project quiet dignity with overlapping layers of concern. He faced the door as all good predators do. She sat to his right. He held her hand and was stroking the side of her face. She was dissociating. That's what prey animals do. It's a protective mechanism. It plays out this way. If the prey animal can sit still long enough, maybe they don't get hurt. Maybe.

I sat across from Staci and to his left. I kept my eyes fixed on Staci. I wanted to connect with her. She needed to know she was safe, that I would not allow anything more to happen to her.

"I understand it's been a strenuous morning. Can you tell me what's been happening?"

The tears became bigger and the large man's barrel chest heaved heavily. "I love her. I love you, Staci. I am so sorry, honey. I never wanted to hurt you."

"I understand you love her and you didn't want to hurt her, but can you tell me what's been going on here?"

Staci remained somewhere in space. That was good. It was protective. She was going to break the hysterical barrier at some point. Best not here, not now.

"Why did you have a gun?"

Staci blinked and moved her face toward his. "You promised you'd talk to him."

The story started haltingly accompanied by more tears. As he continued the story became rote and had a tinny, well-rehearsed quality. The tears disappeared. He stopped talking occasionally to see if Staci was listening. He was on stage and he wanted the audience's full attention. "I did it only because I love you, Staci."

He had threatened to kill Staci many times during their marriage. On several occasions he had taken Staci into the woods and marched her to the same spot. He'd announce, "This is where you will die." It turned out these were practice runs.

Driven by what he perceived as love and great

grief and loss, he had broken the restraining order and gone to their home to kill Staci. He knew her routine and was determined she would never walk out of their house again. He sat down along the wood line south of their home. From a distance of a hundred feet, he put his scope on her. He had clear shots at her in the bedroom and the bathroom. He followed her movements from room to room. He put pressure on the trigger twice. He watched her shower and dress. It was perverse. He took his finger off the trigger and just watched. He decided she needed to die slowly and she needed to see his face as she died. When Staci left the house to get into her car, he jumped from behind her as she fumbled for her keys. He threw her to the ground and punched and kicked her. He choked her until her eyes became distant and her breath paused.

He pulled her to her feet and, hitting her with the butt of his rifle, marched her into the woods to their special place. It was a mile hike in the dark winter morning. He extolled his love and condemned her for her manipulations. He described to her his fantasies. This was not going to be an easy death. She had debts to pay. He laughed at some of the brutality.

Once at the site, he changed the plan. He pushed her into the snow, tore her clothes off, and raped her, just for the humiliation. He bit her. He slapped her. He made fun of her weakness. He ordered her to dress. She sat with her arms around her knees. He stood behind her with the rifle at her head and ordered her to pray. He teasingly encouraged her to cry. His mantra was "This is your fault. You're making me do this. If you only loved me."

She had remained silent and resolute. In a trembling whisper the words almost silently escaped on her breath. The words were more painful than her fear of death. "I love you. This is my fault. I should have loved you more. I know now how much you mean to me." She had drilled with a coworker what she would do in this situation. She began acting and the words rolled out.

She was terrified and hoping for a quick end. He put the gun down and embraced her. She had come to her senses. He could love her again. He held her and caressed her. She needed medical attention. She convinced him that they would be okay. They needed a story. He needed help. They needed help. They would be okay. She promised no police. She convinced him I was safe. They came to share their story.

I kept my eyes on Staci. She sobbed quietly but did not move. She was frozen in fright. When he finished, she looked to the floor in shame. I marveled at her strength.

"She's had a tough day, but then so have you. I see how much you love her. You must feel awful about today." Like a good sociopath he bit on the next line. "If you are feeling so bad that you might hurt yourself, I could put you in the hospital."

"I hate what I've done, man. I just want to die. I want to kill myself."

MENTAL HEALTH DAYS

"Do you want to go to the hospital so you can be safe?"

"Yeah, please help me. I love her so much."

I assured him and Staci they would be all right. I left the room to call the hospital. I alerted staff to the situation and asked that they make the call. When I reentered the room, he held Staci tightly and was crying. She was limp. I took her hand. "Everything's been worked out. Everything's okay."

As he and I left for the hospital, he begged for her to visit. "You've got to come, Staci. I'll go but I'm doing it for you. You have to swear you will come and visit. Tonight. I want to see you tonight." As we walked down the hall, staff rushed in to take care of Staci.

I took him to the emergency room for evaluation. I took the doctor aside and gave him the full story. The doc talked to him and got the same details. He also parroted for the doc that he wasn't feeling safe and needed to be hospitalized. He was taken to the psych unit and given drugs to calm him down. The cops were called when he was most amenable to arrest.

I hurried back to the office. Staci was there, being interviewed by the police. She was surrounded by female staff, and they bathed her with real love and care. Staci laughed with them as they talked about their rehearsals. Staci needed a great performance and she delivered. I went to the car to get Staci's coat. The rifle lay in the backseat, uncased, unfired. I relaxed and felt an urge to wet myself.

Dan: The Man with the Plan

HE WAS A dichotomy from the beginning. He could show the greatest compassion to the homeless vets he worked with, but then he'd trash them as weak and corrupt, lesser human beings. Sometimes he was a lean, mean athlete who could ride his bike for a hundred miles on a sunny day and then he'd give in to his demons and become drunk for months and turn into a reddish blob of a man. He didn't trust men, but he could make women swoon over such a "sensitive" man. The plan, his plan, was simply genius. One day he would just disappear. He'd vanish and no one would know if he had drifted down to New Orleans to sell hot dogs from a cart on Bourbon Street or was sitting under a large pine tree with a self-inflicted gunshot wound to the head.

The plan had been long in the making. He grew up dirt poor where the only thing harder than the floor

DAN: THE MAN WITH THE PLAN

he slept on was the sting of his father's fist. He hid in the woods and played in the treetops. He developed a unique skill. He would climb to the top of the tallest pines and begin the great tree's swaying. As the green needles of one pine reached across space to shake hands with the next tree, he'd leap. When the time for escape came, he'd flee to Canada, one tree at a time.

He was an outcast by age six—dirty, poorly clothed, bruised, and socially inept. Other children mocked him. He learned to avoid everyone. He came to believe he was invisible. He walked among the living, but no one noticed. When he was finally seen, he slurped up the attention like melted ice cream. Local toughs, the cool guys with fast cars and faster women, took a shine to him. He ran their errands and polished their cars. They were high school dropouts, and he was a grade school runaway. He was accepted into the club and became their sex toy. It hurt at first. Then he learned to go numb. After many years of being their pleasure cushion, he felt nothing but shame. The shame festered and rage grew from the cancerous green ooze of deep-seated self-loathing.

He joined the Army to get out of town and to travel and see exotic places and get himself killed. He didn't have the courage to self-destruct. He needed others' help. Constantly intoxicated when not at war, he served four tours in Vietnam. He would walk point at every opportunity. He volunteered to be a tunnel rat. He'd enter underground complexes hiding the enemy.

He'd go head first, armed with a flashlight and a pistol to ferret out the Cong hiding in the darkness. He was angry on discharge. He gave Charlie four years of his life so that they could end it. They failed.

Between his second and third tours, he went home on leave. He sat at a small tavern deep in the woods drinking himself into oblivion. The Cool Guys from his past showed up. Dan had become invisible again. They did not see him. Dan went outside to piss. He loosened the lug nuts on the left front tire. The Cool Guys left that night leaning on each other. Too drunk to walk, they drove to their deaths. On a tight curve the wheel flew off, and three men died. When drunk and feeling morose, Dan would pull out a newspaper clipping that announced his work had prevailed.

Our relationship became as rocky as the forest roads. He left before I could fire him. He was still angry. I believe he felt shame at having failed again. Two days later I was driving home, when on a curve my car fell to the pavement and my left front tire went sailing into a swamp. Coincidence?

Years later I was invited to join the board of directors of a local nonprofit that specialized in helping victims of human violence. My first meeting I sat across from the board chairman. Dan shook my hand. Across that table we renewed our acquaintance. He talked little outside the meetings, but I did find out he still put one paycheck a month in a sock. The sock went into his sock drawer with many other socks full

DAN: THE MAN WITH THE PLAN

of money. The money was the foundation of his plan.

The last time I saw Dan, he was staggering down the main street. He was walking point, following the tunnels from one bar to the next, daring the gooks one more time. He died shortly after that sighting. There are times I close my eyes and I dream of Carnival time in New Orleans. I'm walking along with a beer in my hand and a deep hunger in my stomach. I walk to Jackson Square and on the far side is a hot dog wagon. Dan waves me over.

Dancing with Bears

YOU SHOULD HAVE heard his roar! It came from the depths of Hell and exploded from his lips like the magma from Vesuvius. He is silenced now. Not a whimper. Death does that.

This great bear of a man stalked the streets. The menace of his walk and the swagger of his smile made children scream and women scatter. He carried his pain like a great lance, willing to pierce friend or foe alike when they tripped his shame of surviving. The abuse put upon him did not make him stronger; it instilled in him an unquenchable shame and a seething anger. Touch those twin engines of rage and the price to be paid was the humbling of one's soul and the searing of one's psyche. You were lucky if his pain was just planted on you physically.

I stood up to him. He didn't back down. He circled and growled. I stayed out of reach and put my hands up to signal no weapon, no threat. He led, I followed. We twirled. He bobbed and I weaved. The dance was static. Then he gave a great harrumph and it ended. He walked back to his sanctuary growling in his madness. I let out a great breath and felt the need to fall to my knees, but when dancing with bears, you can't show weakness. This is how we met.

He learned to tolerate me, and I learned to respect him. Over the years we begrudgingly came to understand that we were made from the same human cloth. His abuse took him in one direction, and I was fortunate to grow in another. Over time he would let a small crack in his thick defensive walls develop, and small feats of kindness spilled forth. At first he would quickly mortar these cracks so he did not feel exposed and weak. Each small act of goodness built upon the next, and his growl became a low rumble. His muscles relaxed and his smile evolved. He became human. He shared his humor and his poetry. I laughed and I cried. His pain touched my heart and I grew within, embracing his hate and his love. Both came without pretentions. It was real. It was raw.

He called because he was dying. I went to him in the hospice, and we engaged in our dance. "How come you became my friend," asked a man who had spent most of his adult life caged like an angry bear.

Afraid to share my heart, I answered, "My dad was a sheriff; I'm used to ex-cons. You don't scare me."

"Is that all you think of me?"

"No, what I meant to say is that I've known hard, crusty men all my life. On the inside, most of them were like you, marshmallows."

He laughed.

The pain from his cancer became overwhelming, and he was put on a regimen of sedation that stole his consciousness. He had brief moments when we would speak. He asked at the end each visit, "Are you my friend?" and he would hold out his great paw for me to take.

My last visit I entered as he slept. I watched. There's this evolutionary adaptation all mammals have made that allows the brain to attach to another creature and to accept that creature unconditionally. It's called the mammalian face. All mammal infants (like humans) have these large round faces, with high foreheads and great big eyes. When we see this face, we are programmed to go "Oh, a puppy…a kitty…a baby," and we can't help ourselves. We fall in love.

He winced in pain and he awoke. His eyes were enlarged by the lenses of his glasses, and they played against the baldness of his forehead. He smiled, childlike, and I was triggered. "Oh, a baby, a teddy bear!" He made me smile.

Nothing important was said. No great insights were shared. He faded in and out, and I just smiled to reassure him I was still there. I made my exit when he was conscious. I looked down upon him and promised to return. He had lost the use of his right arm. His hand jerked as I began to walk away. His fingers flexed. I took his hand and squeezed it. "Friend," I said, and he smiled.

Destiny and Great Love

ALL GREAT LOVES are destined. Romeo and Juliet. Antony and Cleopatra. Bonnie and Clyde. Madonna… and you fill in the blank. Destiny and great love once struck me. They both should have gotten the maximum for assault and battery.

When I was a college sophomore, hormones had mugged my better senses and sent me careening down romantic roads best left untraveled. Once such path led me to Mary. She was a goddess. Golden tresses to the middle of her back. Her eyes were soft and inviting, and her smile ignited explosions of testosterone.

I had long admired her from a distance. I was enchanted, but my adoration kept me from speaking to her. I went into full cardiac arrest when she asked me to the winter formal.

The grand nature of the date complicated things. I needed to get over my shyness and I needed a quick plan to exit my poverty. Flowers and dinner were mandatory. Money was in short supply. I needed advice and wisdom from a real sage. Instead, I turned to a friend.

We put together a strategy, simple but romantic. The lack of money was replaced by style and grace. A single red rose and a candlelight dinner in the dorm room would overcome my doubts of an unsuccessful date.

On the day of the big dance, I was shaking in anticipation. Buff, my friend (named after the animal which shared the same large head of hair), helped me clean my car of empty beverage cans and moldy textbooks. We drove into town early. Buff suggested a little nerve tonic. One tonic led to two, two became three…!

I was to pick Mary up at her dorm on the Catholic women's campus. Still reeling and stumbling from my confidence-boosting session, I tumbled getting out of the car. The door slammed on the single red rose. The bud fell into the passenger seat. I stood a thorny stick in my hand.

Shaken, but not deterred, I walked with a slight stagger to the dorm's reception desk. I asked the head nun for benediction and some tape. The rose was reconstructed with tape, a paper clip, and a prayer.

I asked the good sister for directions to Mary's room. Her hand hovered over a large ruler. She kissed her crucifix, made the Sign of the Cross, said something in Latin, and pointed me down the hall.

Mary came to the door resplendent in a full-length

black crushed velvet dress she had sewn herself. I handed her the surgically repaired rose. She gracefully raised the flower to her dainty nostrils. The tape gave and I praised God she didn't poke herself in the eye with the stem. "A rose is a rose," I quickly countered.

Buff had improvised a dinner. A table borrowed from the student lounge, an almost clean bedsheet, and a candle from the chapel created the ambiance I sought. We settled into the romantic dinner and gazed into each other's eyes. Buff served dinner on dishes liberated from the student café. The meal was four courses, just coincidentally the same four being served in the student rectory. The air was charged. Mary and I were enraptured.

Buff served dessert, strawberry shortcake with mounds of whipped cream. Buff shared a joke. I laughed and pounded the table. Mary's cake jumped off the table and attached itself to her left breast. Instinctively the gentlemen, Buff and I reached out to her with our napkins. Startled, she screamed and fell from her seat.

Hurried apologies and genuine embarrassment fixed a ticklish situation. Mary and I left for the winter formal. We found ourselves on the dance floor. She fit comfortably in my arms, and we danced slowly to the rhythm of the Temptations, lost in each other's eyes. The magic had returned. We twirled and whirled completely enthralled in the moment. As we executed a delicate step, I felt resistance. I planted my foot firmly and turned. Shock registered in Mary's eyes. Her dress had torn from the bodice and lay beneath our feet.

There were no more recoveries. No more chances for extended apologies. Destiny had struck. Sometimes it is better to live and not love. It saves on the humiliation.

Train of Thought

MY DOGS HOWLING stirred me out of my dreams. The clock was locked on a luminescent 3 a.m. The dogs' howls were mournful and prayerful. The passing ore train answered. The mechanical howl marked the passing of the dark, misty serpent. The heated ore on the train threw hot steam into the air giving the procession a ghostly image as the great iron reptile convulsed and crawled through the night.

Kevin had come into life the same way, writhing and howling, his beauty and sleekness reflected in the eyes of astonished young parents. Kevin was a glorious child. Dark masses of curls fell over his forehead. Deep, dark, darting eyes pulled in the wonders of a new world and a life unlimited.

He, too, had lived by the tracks. The rumbling of the great trains rocked him to sleep as they crossed and re-crossed the great Mesabi Iron Range. His blood flowed to the rhythm of the rails. He learned to walk with a clickety clack. He waved to the passing engineers and convulsed with laughter when they saluted him with a toot. Before he said "dad" it was whoo-whoo-whoo.

When Kevin was a toddler, people spoke of his awkwardness of gait and the developing shyness that dimmed the omnipresent smile. He was becoming tall and lanky, with each limb seemingly moving with an independent mind. Children teased Kevin, and before he was of school age, he knew he was different.

In grade school he was taunted and he withdrew into fantasy. His mind became a sanctuary into which no one was allowed. In junior high the taunts became beatings. Young toughs full of venom struck at the convenient gangling adolescent. Kevin withdrew further and became a specter haunting the hallowed halls of learning.

Desperate for friendship he was unseen by all but the school janitor. The man mentored Kevin, and the janitor's office provided a harbor from the storm. The janitor gave companionship, but he took Kevin sexually.

Ghosts and dreadful apparitions began to appear to Kevin. Voices in his head teased and laughed. Kevin wanted comfort. He turned to drugs and alcohol. He didn't need a prescription to medicate the developing mental illness.

Lost in a trance of demons and devils, Kevin still turned to the great growling trains for comfort. One of those great ghostly, steaming snakes raced from hell on a cold October night. It was 4 a.m. and the ground was releasing its fog. Steam poured from the frozen steel cars. A brilliant starry sky smiled down on the fiery engine and the misty figure of a young boy forgotten.

Kevin peacefully lay on the tracks. In a fetal position he smiled at all the possibilities of life anew. He put his hands over his ears to ward off the taunts and jeers of a life already forgotten. He mocked the voices within his head and ordered them to silence. His body rocked and rolled with the clickety clack.

When the trains run now at night, my dogs still howl and the trains blast their whistles in response, but on the stillest of nights amid the chorus of animal and metal screams, I hear the whimper of a little boy lost, calling out for a friend.

One Cold Winter's Night

SOMETIMES IT'S NOT good to be alone. The mind begins to dwell on things best left in tidy little piles somewhere outside. I was in town today and I ran into a friend. It's not very professional of me to call someone I know solely through work a friend, but I've known her for years. I know all her painful secrets. They are engraved on my brain. She's a native woman. I see her frequently at the Drop-In. I've sat with her through countless crises. She calls me, affectionately, Chester the Molester. I say *affectionately* because that's her pet name for me. She likes to startle my colleagues by referring to me in such glowing terms. She readily smiles as she says it and then breaks into great laughter when she gets the response she is expecting. She's two years younger than I but carries the weight of thousands of years of pain. Her story is familiar for Native American females. Rapes, incest, beatings, and senseless alcoholic stupors to medicate the evil thoughts and keep the spirits of humiliation and shame at bay become a lifestyle.

When I teach social psychology, I spend class periods discussing bias, stereotypes, and prejudice. I use Native Americans as the example as they are the largest minority in northern Minnesota. Most of the students hold many of the old biases. I tell them not to be ashamed; we are all biased. It simply means we don't understand another group of people. I reassure them that being biased doesn't make them bad people, only human. What makes us bad is when we don't learn to turn from those biases and continue to view others according to the stereotypes that dehumanize them. Some student will almost always point out that stereotypes can be true and then use instances of native violence on natives and native drinking as evidence of true stereotypes. These students have never had contact with natives, or they know "one good Indian" who doesn't fit the standard image of the drunken, lazy, and violent native.

They don't understand trauma and how trauma can become the organizing principle of one's life. Trauma can form the norms and traditions of a whole people. Individuals who have been traumatized will often try to gain control of the hurt by repeating the event that brought the pain. They hope to gain mastery over it by repeating it until they get it right. People who have been traumatized lose their spiritual center and are often more willing to hurt and humiliate others. It becomes epidemic. Hurt fosters hurt. Pain births pain.

PLAYING COPS

Sometimes the only thing that stops pain is shifting one's sense of consciousness with alcohol or drugs. These substances hold back the old pains but leave one vulnerable, and often new pain emerges from the incidents that occur when one is self-medicated.

Natives were hunted and killed for sport and for their lands not that many generations ago. We put them on reservations and allowed them to starve to death. Up until the 1960s, we were still stealing their children and putting them in boarding schools to make them white. What is it like to have the knowledge and stories of such a painful past? How do you reconcile that your great-grandparents may have been hunted as animals? What do you do with information that the great white majority felt that nothing in Indian country had value? Alice Miller, an Austrian psychiatrist who researches children and trauma, says, "We are all good people who have been hurt." Natives have held that hurt for many generations, and like all injured people they will pass it on to generation after generation. The cycle is hard for an individual to break. How does an entire people turn away from it?

This past semester when the class was exploring these issues, I had three remarkable crisis calls in one day. I brought these stories to class to humanize the theory.

Early in the day a homeless native woman in her thirties came to the office. Her white boyfriend had drugged her and passed her around as a sexual entrée

ONE COLD WINTER'S NIGHT

to his drunken friends. He then threw her out of the house. She was homeless again for the fourth time in five years. She spoke respectfully of him at first; after all, she was addressing her sorrows to another white man. She was polite in regard to her father too, who had beaten her throughout her childhood. He was never stopped because her mother/his wife had committed suicide when she was six. She had seen the body. No one could protect her, and she knew no one could be trusted. She was raped on the school bus at age twelve by white and native youths. She became rebellious. I should tell you that such behavior is a very common response to trauma. Acting out and pushing back against authority gives one a sense of temporary control and power. She had a succession of boyfriends and husbands, all who degraded her sexually and beat her when she complained. She had four children by four different men, but she loved all her children equally and genuinely. She was now without shelter and needed medical care. She did not trust.

I got a phone call from a coworker to meet with a client of his at her residence. He informed me that she was a native grandmother and that she, her daughter, and her two granddaughters were facing eviction. Grandmother was suicidal. When I arrived I found a woman who was in her mid-fifties. She was very suicidal. She felt she was failing her family. She was overwhelmed with many circumstances beyond her control. She had relapsed and began drinking after years of sobriety. This added to her shame. With her money gone she could not pay the rent or buy groceries for her family. She saw her only option as death.

I sent my coworker to get groceries for the weekend. I began to work with her to reestablish her emotional equilibrium. She was humiliated for having failed her family. She chastised herself for turning to alcohol to resolve her pain. I used all the tricks. I came to a point where I hoped to use her grandchildren to give her strength and a reason to continue on. I pointed out that she had twenty years or more of life to be the role model and good provider to her grandchildren that she wanted so desperately to be. She laughed at me. "You speak from the white man's world." I knew what she meant. Natives tend to die in their mid-fifties from the effects of their social conditions. I had to laugh with her. "Yes," I said, "I just a stupid white man." She howled with delight.

Back at the office I was walking down the hall when a native man in his late thirties asked to speak to me. He was crying. He hid his face so that I would not see that he was not a warrior. He was familiar to me. He had used the Drop-In for meals. I had never known him to seek out staff or to ask for anything. I walked him back to my office. He was cringing and grimacing in great pain. He was also withdrawing from a four-day alcoholic binge. He begged for my help. He cried for assistance. He, too, felt overwhelming humiliation and shame. He needed housing and food. He needed medical attention. He shared he was a felon. At age sixteen he had had sex with a fifteen-year-old cousin. Telling me this information, he shared he had been sexually abused for many years when he was young by a cousin and uncle. When he had shared this family history, he innocently added, "It's not so bad. Doesn't everybody do that?"

His pain was unbroken. He took off his shirt, and his body was covered with deep black bruises. His wrist appeared broken. "Maybe we should get you to a doctor first," I offered.

"No, I don't want to go to the hospital."

"You need to see a doctor."

"I was there last night and they kicked me out."

This engaged my moral indignity. "Why, because you're an Indian?"

Softly, "No, because I'm a drunk."

Stereotypes. I shared these stories with the class so they could see that I still have stereotypes to defeat. So that you may sleep, they all found housing. They continue to struggle with their demons, but they are proud of and own their heritage. They love their children and families. They are looking for love and support. They are all good people who have been hurt.

Snow Rabbit

IN MIDDLE AGE my passion is cross-country skiing. My legs betrayed me long ago. My agility has become questionable. My stamina yields to breathlessness. Yet, when I slide my foot into the ski bindings and push off along a wooded trail, the adrenaline starts pumping and the vigor of youth returns.

During Minnesota's long winters, skiing is the keeper of my soul and sanity. I measure life's purpose in kilometers of forested hills and valleys. I compete against myself. I set internal goals and run races only I envision. I call for the track and push past slower skiers. They don't see my sly grin of victory as I double pole past their stationary figures.

Last week I visited my favorite trail and found only one other vehicle in the parking lot. I stretched as I watched the other skier, a young woman, cross a small meadow and enter the woods. She had good technique and was a strong skier. She furtively glanced over her shoulder in my direction as she entered the

SNOW RABBIT

dark forest. I smiled to myself. She'd be the rabbit. I gave her a ten-minute head start. Then I pushed off with every intention of passing her before she could complete the loop. I could then declare myself the winner and apply a soothing salve to my male ego.

I felt strong, challenged. I ran up the crest of the first hill and descended its far side with the relentlessness of an alpine downhill racer. As I pushed hard my knees began to feel weak and my lungs begged for oxygen. Then I spotted her. She hadn't broken stride and she glided through the woods unimpeded. I picked up my pace.

I started gaining on her as she began climbing the longest hill on the trail. I knew I could close ground on her here. When I reached the long slope, I attacked it like a mad stormtrooper. At the peak I caught sight of her entering the first black spruce bog in the woods. She furtively glanced in my direction and hastened her pace. The rabbit was running. I stopped at the crest of the hill, filled my lungs with the chilled air, and then plunged downward in hot pursuit.

Exiting the bog, I chased her along a barren ridge. Halfway across the ridge, she broke her stride and faltered. I knew I had won. I planned my strategy. I would catch her just before the next descent. I would fly past her with a tip of my hat and disappear down the hill, full of male pride.

I was within yards of her when she collapsed and fell to her knees. As I approached she cowered, and fear filled her eyes. I averted my eyes and continued on without breaking stride. I had not thought of myself as a threat. Nor had I ever thought of what it must sometimes be like to be a woman. I had become one of the thoughtless and hedonistic men who bully to impress. Sometimes we men do it intentionally; other times it's quite innocent. Sometimes the signals get crossed. What we make to be innocent fun can often be interpreted as a threat. What I assumed was just play was a trespass of another's personal boundaries. One woman's fear reminded me of my inconsideration. One woman's terror touched my shame.

Streams of Life

MY WORK IS twenty-five miles from my home. It's a blessing; the ride home is a chance to unwind as I wander through the byways of the north woods. I have an infinite number of routes home. Country roads, forest roads, mining roads, they all lead home.

Flowing among and around these roads, a little stream meanders. I can cross it a dozen different ways. Each crossing reveals new angles of looking at the flow of life. New truths continuously float by.

Early one spring, I surprised the stream as I came over a small knoll. The waters held the legs of a young man. I drove by slowly so not to disturb him. The boy was lost in the grip of the water and did not notice my passing. His thoughts were elsewhere, perhaps flowing with the sweep of the stream and even beyond the containment of the water's banks. Great tears were rolling down his cheeks, mixing with the riffles of the fast-flowing creek and beginning the long journey to the Gulf of Mexico.

Ah, a mystery. Some intrigue. On such a beautiful day, why wasn't the young man matching laughter with the bubbling brook?

Around a wide, slow curve, hidden by a curtain of large swaying pines, came the answer. Young love and passionate love appeared. A young woman walked alone. Her hair swung and bounced with the slow purposefulness of her saddened walk. She held her head down, allowing her tears to reach the dust of the road unencumbered. As I drove past she raised her hands to her face. Why is sadness such a private matter?

Adolescent love—is there ever a time in our lives when greater feelings torment or tear at us? The soul-scorching pains of young love are beyond comprehension. Do we ever recover?

My first love was alphabetically related. We shared initials and our school careers were spent in desks separated by vowels. She sat forever in the desk just in front of me. I did not see her until the spring of my junior year. I was helping decorate the gym for the prom when I noticed these gorgeous legs on the ladder above my head. I looked up into the kindest, most enticing brown eyes and the widest, most inviting smile ever hidden by the alphabet.

It took me two weeks to summon the courage to ask her out. We went to a movie. She wore a sweater of her father's on this cool spring evening. It draped over her shoulders like dew clinging to a petal. At dark I took her home. I walked her to the door of her country house. High anxiety shook me and shot electrical tremors through my limbs. Each step was more dangerous than the next. Each breath heavy with the difficulty of anticipation. At the door it was decision time. Do I go for the first kiss? I hesitated a second too long. She slipped inside. Her loving eyes gazed at me from behind a screen door. I placed my lips against the cool metal and met her sweet lips. I floated away, totally enamored and spitting out flies.

The romance did not survive. It caused me great pain. My heart floundered. No amount of tears seemed able to start the healing, but I survived. Looking back in my car's mirror, I knew the young lovers now so sorrowed would also survive and thrive.

Tomorrow will bring new roads and new stories. The rivers of life will continue to flow. I hope everyone experiences the equal delicacies of first kisses and old flies.

Lessons Learned

"Good teaching is one-fourth preparation and three-fourths theatre." —Gail Godwin

"A good teacher affects eternity; a teacher can never tell where their influence stops."
—Henry Brooks Adams

IT'S A MONTH before the next semester starts. I'm pulling out the old texts, rewriting the syllabus, and preparing for my part-time gig as an adjunct professor of psychology. It's a joy to teach. Most of the students are nontraditional and eager to learn. They're inquisitive and ready to challenge me, so I have to be on top of my game. It forces me to stay current and to continue learning, myself.

Out of high school I had planned on teaching. Someone along the way advised me that the world had too many teachers and too few teaching jobs, so I put teaching on the shelf and drifted through college only knowing I wasn't going to be a teacher.

LESSONS LEARNED

I got my first chance to teach when the community college asked me to take on a Social Problems class twenty years ago. I had no clue how to teach, but I had experience in community theatre, so I developed a little routine from that first day that serves me well yet today. When the last student enters the classroom, I close the door, take a deep breath, and shout out in my head, "It's showtime!" I spin around to face the class and it's on. I simply channel the behaviors of instructors who held my attention and "act" like a teacher. I had no guiding principle or theory of education to lead me. I once had another educator ask me my style of teaching. He was looking for a label. I could only give him a description. Later a student saved me further embarrassment when he declared, "Man, I love your Socratic style." So there you are. I take a Socratic approach to teaching.

That first Social Problems class hooked me on teaching. Two students particularly stood out. The first was a young woman in her early twenties. She had a dark olive complexion and wonderfully black curly hair. She sat in the back of the room and rarely participated in discussion. She did listen intently.

Her counterpart was a young tough who sat up front and challenged everything I or the text presented. He dressed like a biker. He had the leather and chains. He wore a beard and long, distressed tresses of hair. I loved the guy. He didn't argue to be argumentative. He argued to see every angle of a question, to dissect and discern every idea. He had a great sense of humor and used it to keep everyone's defenses down. He said he was lost and wasn't sure what he wanted out of life. He was in school to find himself.

Social Problems was a great class. We discussed everything from racism to the causes of war. During our discussion of racism and discrimination, I used the local Native American population as an example. I asked for examples of student travels and the reasons they traveled. Simplified, many said they liked to travel to see and experience other cultures. I used that and asked how many had ever been to the Bois Forte Reservation, only forty miles away. None had, and many were not acquainted with the formal name of the Rez. This led to a wonderful discussion of the cultural differences between the traditional world of the native population and the culture of white rural America.

The whole semester was a constant learning experience for myself and the class. The trust and openness in class allowed for great questions and long, deliberative discussions. I hated to see the class end. On the last night, I was sad to see the students file out. I stood at the door and thanked each student for participating and making the class such a wonderful experience for me. When I turned back to the class, the young woman with the olive complexion and black curly hair was still seated. She quietly gathered her books and came to my desk. She spent ten minutes thanking me. I had thought she was Italian, but her mother was white and her father was native. She shared that her father had left the family when she was very young. Her mother had never lost an opportunity to talk ugly and degradingly of Native Americans. She whimpered quietly when she talked about feeling so much shame for her entire life, simply because she was native. She told me I was the first person she had ever heard say positive things about natives. She wanted to thank me for the opportunity to feel some pride in who she was. I was almost moved to tears as she silently glided out the door.

I picked up my books and stepped into the hallway. My "biker" student was waiting. He was all smiles and full of enthusiasm. He just had to tell me that he had decided he was going to be a teacher. He needed to share that he wanted to be just like me.

Those were powerful moments that have not been repeated in every class, but it was the drug that got me addicted to teaching. I can't kick the habit.

The Gift

FOR MORE THAN twenty-five years, it was my privilege to share in the grace and humility of so many individuals who had been disabled by severe and persistent mental illness. When I was asked to do community trainings, people would invariably respond, "You must be a patient man" or "How kind you must be." They seemed to believe my profession had been demanding and stressful. To the contrary, I had the opportunity to meet some of the kindest, most extraordinary people who offered me so much and taught me even more. The tears and laughter we shared changed me. From those who had so little, I learned charity; from those whose lives seemed to have been strangled in their development, I learned hope; and from those who seemed to drift friendless, I was given spirituality. I admired how the daily struggles of some, accomplished so valiantly, gave me heart and courage. I must thank them for their compassion and grace toward me.

THE GIFT

To you who have not been graced with the presence of those who struggle to survive on a daily basis, I would like to share the memories I have of three of these fine folks. They all died the same summer. They were companions on the strange journey of life. They survived and thrived together. In one season their lives ended.

Allen was married following graduation from high school. He attended a community college, had two sons, and started a career in sales. He was pursuing and succeeding in the American Dream.

Allen's mental illness did not suddenly envelop him as it had others. It pursued him and slowly crept into his brain. Patiently, inexhaustibly, his mind became a stranger to him. Fear and suspicion became his constant companions. The voices in his head shadowed his life with warnings about strangers and loved ones. Those closest to him became his enemies. Rambling, incoherent thoughts stole his ability to comprehend and make sense of the world around him.

His small family was thrust into poverty. Friends and family withdrew from them. They were on a whirlwind ride of madness with no one to catch them. They gathered their strength and attempted to nurture and support Allen, but they, too, were eventually pulled down, and Allen was left alone with a small government check designed to keep him steeped in poverty, a room rented in the worst corner of the community, and a family of dreams crushed.

Allen gallantly fought daily to regain the normalcy of life. He mechanically took his medications. He enrolled in rehabilitation programs. He attempted work during the times his thoughts were clear. Several times he seemed to get to the top of the mountain, only to discover a precipice and to fall even farther into the crevasses of his illness.

In the twenty-eighth year of his life, Allen gathered all his resources and made one last charge at normalcy. He contacted his estranged family and began forging new bonds. He converted to Catholicism and struggled late into the nights learning the tenets of his new church. It seemed he would grasp a new fact, his brain would scramble it, and Allen would struggle to un-code it anew. Allen was steeped in grace on the day of his baptism. After the ceremony he imbibed in a simple meal with his family. They parted following hugs and promises of new days. Allen returned to his small room.

His body was found three days later. Complaints had been made about odors from his room. Management had checked. Autopsy could find no definitive cause. His was just a quiet death in an unappreciated life.

Janelle graduated valedictorian of her high school class. She attended a small, elite, private college and again gained top honors. Seeking adventure she traveled to Europe. She gained a job writing for *Stars and Stripes*. She had made a home as an international traveler and writer, and she was enjoying her Bohemian

THE GIFT

lifestyle. But her mental illness swept over her like a tsunami. She drowned in its crushing waves of distorted thoughts and images. She became lost in Europe, living on trash and sympathy. She was arrested for vagrancy and deported back to the States. She wandered across her home country following the paranoia of her illness. It led her to rapes and beatings as common as sunsets.

I only heard Janelle share this story one time. Her words were spoken quietly, dispassionately. She was at a community event designed to educate her neighbors. Following her remarks, between bites of a cookie I heard one of the audience share knowingly with another, "That girl is so delusional." Janelle's diagnosis, her label, robbed her of the truth of her own life. Janelle had been dead ten days before she was even missed. She, too, died quietly and so alone.

Kevin was raucously funny. Laughter brought him friends and kept his demons away. Kevin had studied engineering prior to his illness and had a fine brain, very analytical and penetrating in its operation. After his illness invited itself in, Kevin's brain had its great cynical humor and its devils.

Kevin lived alone. Flophouses were his domain. Kevin preferred solitude and had to be enticed to take part in a world he found tense and threatening. Monsters unseen lurked around all corners.

Kevin had taken medications most of his adult life. They kept the monsters at bay. He resisted the meds as he insisted they poisoned him. In good faith the system wore him down and kept him medicated. The medications gave Kevin days of lucidity and clarity. The medications were also toxic and deadly. The line between therapeutic dosage and toxicity was thin and tenuous.

Kevin went to the ER one evening. He walked more than a mile in the heat of a sultry night. He had been having hot and cold sweats. His muscles were cramping, causing great pain, and his thirst was incurable. At the hospital he gave a full history, including his mental illness and medication regimen. A nurse relayed the information to the attending physician. Kevin was showing classic symptoms of lithium poisoning. The doctor did not even have to see Kevin. The diagnosis was clear: MENTAL ILLNESS. Kevin was given aspirin and sent home. He was found dead just inside the door of his apartment the next morning. He had survived his mental illness, but stigma and prejudice killed him.

All three had lived tragic lives. However, they did live better than they died. Hope marked their lives, and apathy marked their graves. They all struggled with illnesses that science and medicine cannot cure. They did transcend those illnesses. They offered friendship, understanding, and compassion to others. They never lost their empathy.

So, no, I am not a patient or kind man. I have received empathy, and having received it, I try to share gracefully the gift bestowed upon me.

We Be In Louisiana

HE SAT RIGIDLY, his back stiffly embracing the chair. Large crocodile tears washed his cheeks. His dark protruding eyes betrayed his fear. His mother sat to his right and behind him. She leaned forward to gain my attention. "Mr. Gary, your pen. He's afraid of your pen." When interviewing people I nervously twirl my pen. "It's your pen," she repeated. "He's afraid your pen is a weapon."

I looked down, dumbfounded, and placed the pen on the desk. "See, I would not hurt you. I'm sorry I frightened you."

I couldn't imagine the fear this man felt. He was thirty-seven years old and had just completed eleven years in prison. He sat before me frozen in terror. "Your mother tells me you have voices."

He smiled broadly. The river of tears was diverted to the corners of his mouth. Softly he spoke. "They are my friends." The tension in his face melted.

I turned to his mother. "How long has he had

voices? When did you sense that he spoke, when he had conversations and no one was there?"

"He always played by himself. He...he always be a loner. Kids were always afraid of him. He never had any friends. He was five or six when he told me his voices were his friends."

"Didn't anybody see this in school? Was he ever diagnosed with any kind of problem in school? Was he ever put on medication?"

"We are in Louisiana. The schools there don't care. They don't care about kids. Since Katrina it's only gotten worse. They got teachers who don't like kids. Unless you ask for help, they don't see the trouble your kid is in. You got to have money to get your kids help."

"Michael," I said as I gently turned back to the terrified man, "when you were in prison, did you see a doctor? Did anyone give you medication? Have you been told that you have a mental illness?"

The words were formed very slowly and spoken with an uncommon gentleness. "I was afraid all the time in prison. I kept to myself. Prison is dangerous. I stayed in my cell all the time and talked with my friends."

"Do you mean the voices in your head?"

"Yes, they're good to me. I played with them when I was a kid." He drew back; a flash of fear sparked his eyes. "Some of the voices are good. Some of the voices are bad."

"Michael, your mother has told me that you were in prison for assault and weapon charges. The voices, have they ever told you to hurt anyone?"

"The bad voices. The bad voices tell me to do things."

Michael's mother cleared her throat and raised her hand as if she needed permission to speak. "He was in prison for having a weapon when he was on probation. He was a felon. You can't be a felon and have a gun. But he was afraid. He was always afraid. He thinks the spirits are going to get him."

"Michael, can you tell me what your mother means by spirits? Do you see things that others may not see?"

"At night, that's why I can't sleep at night. Coming to get me. They always come at night."

I sat back. "You mean to tell me that this man was imprisoned for eleven years, and no one thought to help him. No one sent him to the doctor. No one gave him medications." I wasn't speaking to anyone in particular.

"We be in Louisiana," his mother remarked. "When you is in prison in Louisiana, people don't care if you even die. They are not going to give you any doc to see or medications. You there to be in prison and just prison. In Louisiana, they don't treat people like people. You got to have money to see a good doctor. If you don't have money, doctor won't even listen to you. If you got money, they'll ask you questions. They will give you medication.

"You be good people up here. You treat people like people. My friends said you'd be a good man, Dr. Gary; you'd listen and you'd help us." She looked out the window. The beginnings of a new six inches of snow had begun to fall. She smiled. Michael smiled. "We not be in Louisiana." Tears be mixing with the snow.

Can You Hear Me Now

THE PHONE RINGS.

Hello, this is Gary.

Gary, this is Deb. I called you, you know, last week about getting a second opinion on my head. I'm so fucking pissed. You know that retard said it was all in my head. It's not all in my head. I'm having dizzy spells, I see pixels, and you know those little black dotty things that fly all over. He said it's in my head. They did an MRI and couldn't see nothing. He had these stupid fucking students with him. How stupid is that. What the hell would a fucking college student know? I want you to look up… I want you to get on to your computer and look up… He says there's nothing wrong with me, that it's all in my head. I get these headaches and they're getting worse. What the fuck does…

Deb…

He's an idiot. I'm passing out; my headaches are getting worse.

Deb.

What do you call it? You know. Get on your computer.

Deb, Deb, slow down. What are you talking about? I didn't understand what you said. What is it the doctor can't find?

Head trauma! He said it's all in my head. You know how many times I've been beaten up. That fucker Stan beat me with a baseball bat, how many times. He hit me in the head. I thought I was dead. I mean I should be dead. He can't see anything and he says it's all in my head. Fuck him. I'm going to Duluth and I'm getting a second opinion. I am going to go. I'm just waiting for my brother. My brother wants me to live with him. I'm going to Duluth; then I'm going to get a second opinion. I want to get my brother into treatment. He needs to go to treatment. I haven't used for two years. He needs me. He needs to get into treatment. And then that stupid doctor…

Deb… Deb… Deb. Slow it down. I'm not sure what you're saying to me. The doctor said what's all in your head.

He doesn't believe me. He thinks I'm making it up. I almost died from how many beatings. I have headaches, and sometimes I just stare straight ahead. I'm like in a trance and I can't get out of it. He says he can't find anything that the x-rays, the MRI doesn't show anything. How can I be lying? It's getting worse and it's going to kill me. I don't want to die. I don't

CAN YOU HEAR ME NOW

want this to kill me. That fucker Stan hit me with a bat. He's winning if I die. I should go kill the fucker. Why is that doctor saying I'm making this up? You can't always see these things. They're invisible. Get on your computer and look it up. Closed head trauma. You can't always see it and then it kills you. I have a level one, but it's getting worse. I could be level two, and level three kills you. I don't want to die. Everyone around me dies. My mom died young. My aunt May died young. I was going to visit her and she died. It's like anything I touch, anyone I try to help, they die. It's me. God is punishing me. What did I do? It's not my fault. That fucking Bruce Johnson, you know, the sheriff, he fucked me. He did this to me. So why is God hurting me.

Deb. Deb. Slow it down. The doctor said he can't see anything wrong in your head. Did you say they did an MRI and the doctor told you he can't see any damage?

He said it's in my head. He thinks I'm a liar. Why would I lie about this? I'm dying. It's going to kill me. I'm having headaches, I go blind, and I get so dizzy I can't even sit up.

Deb. Listen to me. He may not be saying you're a liar. Now I want you to listen.

I want to go to Duluth and…

Deb. Listen. Sometimes when people have been hurt very bad, like you, when people have known nothing but pain and they can't talk about it, then their head needs to make sense of it. Your brain needs to express how awful, how much pain you have. Sometimes what the brain does is make other parts of the body feel the pain that you can't talk about. It's called psychosomatic illness. No one is calling you a liar. What the doctor might be saying is that he does not see any damage to your brain. Physical damage. He may be saying all the symptoms you are reporting are psychosomatic.

He's a stupid…

Deb. Please listen. You have never talked to anyone about these things. You call me and share bit and pieces, so I kind of know what you're talking about. Sometimes when people like you have been hurt and they can't talk about it, the brain needs to find a way to express that pain. You experience the pain and symptoms as real, but your body doesn't show any signs of damage. Your brain has all its signals crossed. Your brain is telling you that you need to talk to someone. Do you understand what I'm trying to say to you? No one is saying you're a liar. What I want you to think about is, is it possible that your brain is producing all these symptoms because you keep all your pain bottled up inside.

You know I can't talk to anyone. They think I'm crazy. I can read people. I know people real well. You know what I've been through. You know I have to be able to know people. I need to know right away if I can trust them. I don't leave my apartment anymore.

I don't trust anyone. I told a lady one time and she laughed at me. She might have been nervous, but she laughed.

I know, Deb. She wasn't laughing at you. It's like you said, she may have been nervous. She may not have ever heard a story quite like yours.

Yeah, but she laughed. She laughed and she said, "I understand." You know how I hate that. She can't understand. She's not me. How can she understand? All that shit fucked me up. It's fucked me up for life.

Deb. She wasn't laughing at you. Sometimes even professionals don't understand. Let me run this by you. You know how many times you've been hurt. You know how that pain never leaves you. You're not crazy. You're not a bad person. You are a person who has been injured. All the crazy thoughts, all the wild behavior—that's very normal for someone who has experienced everything you have experienced. Do you understand?

Kind of.

Deb. See if this makes sense. Sometimes people who have had experiences like you tell me that they get into all kinds of crazy shit behavior, like you. You know how you live on the edge. The prostitution and the stripping. People tell me a couple of things about that kind of behavior. They tell me they did it because it made them feel like they were in control. You know how when you were a kid and people were doing all those awful things to you and you couldn't control those adults. Maybe now you do those things to try and get some control over what happened in the past. Does that make any sense?

Yeah. You know when I was stripping, I did feel like I had some control. They could look, but they couldn't touch me. I knew what they wanted, but I wasn't going to give them any. You know. They're all assholes. I haven't had sex since I moved here. I mean Gene doesn't even get any. I don't feel like it. I feel just numb inside. I liked to have sex with Gene, but I don't feel it. I'm numb. That fucking Stan and all those assholes. They killed it in me. I feel dirty and numb. Gene's been patient. But you know, he's really jealous. He always wants to know who I'm talking to. What I'm doing.

That's okay. You own your body now. No one has a right to tell you what to do with it. It's yours and you have every right to make the rules and set some boundaries. I'm proud of you.

Why does everyone I know die? I get close to someone and they die. I think I kill them. It's like I get to like someone, I want to spend time with them, and they die. Every time. Even my mom left me early. She left me. I was a baby and she left me. Why would she leave me? She must have known I was no good. She left. Then my aunt died and my grandma died. Everyone dies. I'm killing them.

Deb. Slow down. That's magical thinking. Kids use magical thinking to try and understand things that they have no control over. It's like your mom was an alcoholic and drug addict. She wasn't ready or able

CAN YOU HEAR ME NOW

to raise a family. So she ran away. It was her. She's the problem, not you. You were a baby.

I know. But it hurts. I want my mom. I just want someone to love me. That's why I went into dancing. I made a lot of money and I just wanted my dad to be proud of me. But he was ashamed. I destroyed his world. He won't talk to me.

Deb.

No one likes me. I just want to be loved. It's my turn to be loved. I give to everyone. I nursed my dad after he had a bad car accident. I quit dancing for months to stay with my aunt before she died. I'm always helping my brother. He's only a half-brother. But I want to help him. I'm always helping people. Why can't they love me? Why can't someone take care of me?

Deb. Let me try this on you. I've been told by other people who have been in your circumstances that sometimes all this helping is about not having to take a close look at oneself. You know, if you spend all your time fixing other people, then you never have to look at yourself.

Yeah. I know. I can't stand counseling. People don't know me. I can read their body language. I know when they don't like me or think I'm lying. I can see it in their faces.

Deb. Your guard is way up. It's like your antenna is really finely tuned for the slightest hint of rejection. Could it be that maybe people haven't heard a story quite as bad as yours and they are reacting to your pain, and that they're not laughing at you?

It could be. But I can't go to see anyone. I can't leave here. I feel like everyone is looking at me and they can see I have this power to hurt and they don't like me. I can't get out of here. It's scary. Too many people and they're all looking at me.

Deb. Listen. I have an intern working here. She's really good. She can go to your home. She could meet you at your place. I can direct her. She can tell me what's happening with you, and I can give her clues of how to work with you. Would you be willing to try that? Her name is Keran. She's very nice. Would you let her come to your place?

She can come over. I'd like that. But you have to tell her not to say "I understand." She says that and I'm kicking her ass out of here now.

I know. I understand.

Stop that.

All right. Here's what I want you to do. You go to Duluth and get your second opinion. We need to make sure that there is nothing physically wrong with you. You will do that, won't you?

Yes. I want to go see my brother. I can go next week.

Good, I will send Keran over. Can I give her your number?

Yeah.

Can I call you if I need to talk?

Any time.

A Christmas Reflection

I WALKED THE streets of my hometown last night. The houses and trees were flocked with new fallen snow. The lights and sounds of Christmas created a shadow land of joy and color. My attention alternated between the dazzling Christmas displays and the hard crunch of the snow. My mind drifted between the lines of Dickens' *Christmas Carol* and the news and activities of the day.

As the families of the community ready for the presents and celebration, little expense is spared. Everywhere great garlands of colored lights decorate the houses and streets. All manner of businesses and organizations plan and execute their holiday parties. Individuals and families overextend themselves one more time as they search for perfect gifts. Peace and goodwill are the common greeting.

The Salvation Army's bell peels through the night. It's a reminder of Dickens' solicitors asking Scrooge for "a slight provision for the poor." A slight provision, a small intrusion, a tiny show of concern for the less fortunate. At Christmas we all manage to find heart.

An errant paper blows across the street. It contains more than one reference to welfare reform. Those reforms are not even in place. Society's safety net has not yet been cut. Yet in meeting after meeting, I hear that the soup kitchen is seeing many new faces, the homeless shelter has greater numbers, and the emergency funds are being rapidly depleted.

Take heart, for it's the nineties. The credo is no more victims. Our attitudes could not have been summed up any better than Scrooge's reply to the solicitors: "Are there no prisons and the workhouses, are they still in operation? The treadmills and the poor laws are in full vigor then."

Earlier in the day I had attended a meeting with a representative from a managed health care firm regarding funding of mental health care. I had hoped to hear the words of Jacob Marley's ghost as he tried to persuade Scrooge to see beyond the issues of money and business. "Every man who lives should give and share in fellowship with other men."

Instead I heard a man say his company was not interested in "cures or improvement." I listened, smiled, and, conditioned like everyone else to the coldness of business, I smiled and nodded appropriately.

All care providers walked away from the meeting shaking their heads in disgust. We entered into the conspiracy of absolution with the words "it's just business." We had forgotten the full words of Jacob Marley: "Business! Mankind was my business. The common welfare was my business. Charity, mercy, patience, kindness were all my business."

My joy in this season is tempered with a growing anger. Everywhere the callousness of our times is cemented in action and words. We turn from our social responsibilities and hide behind epitaphs of personal responsibility only as it applies to "those others" getting their lives right.

The Ghost of Christmas Present showed Scrooge the children of poverty. Scrooge, forced to view reality, asked, "Are they stray dogs?" Christmas Present replied, "They may as well be for what they lack in care and love." Scrooge, denying responsibility, inquired who they belonged to. The Spirit became enraged. "They are Man's and they are the greatest perversion of mankind."

As I point my finger at others who I blame for the growing disparity in wealth, the wind blows harshly in my face. As Marley's ghost so incriminatory quizzed, "Would you know the weight and length of the chain you bear yourself?" Merry Christmas.

Autumn Blue

THE SKY IS sunny and the air crisp. As birds flock and roadside flowers bloom, I think of a death. The thoughts come in a sequence of nouns that lead to a hollowing of the heart. Wild blue flowers, dancing yellow flowers, roadside beauty, air rarified, Carl, death unbecoming.

Carl was in his early thirties, maybe a little more. Hard telling. Cherub is how I would describe him. He had dark Italian good looks. His mental illness gave him the timid shyness of a fawn. His large brown eyes reflected the frightened child trapped inside.

Carl came into the world with all the promise that would make a momma proud. He was beautiful, intelligent, and gifted with the voice of an angel. As a preteen he would sing in the Chicago opera. His physical beauty matched the voice that would take him to magical places. Somewhere in that universe, during a moment of ugly nastiness, a sexual thing happened that froze Carl in time. Forever he would become a

AUTUMN BLUE

frightened boy who had no control of his pain and fear. He spent the rest of his life a painfully shy child looking for a savior.

I met this man/child when he moved with his mother to the north woods of Wisconsin. He sat in his counseling session upright and rigid, his eyes darting everywhere, his body tense and reacting to each movement I made. I took his hand and it was warm and damp. His limp arm pumped with my handshake, offering the meekest resistance of a victim.

I fell into the rhythm of speech I would use with a child. I slowed and simplified my words. He just smiled and let his mother respond. I wanted to lean over and pat his shoulder and assure him that he needn't be afraid of those things in the dark.

We met weekly and he began to speak in a hesitant, timid voice. He laughed at my jokes and I cried at his violations. He seemed to enjoy our sessions. He began to stand outside my office most evenings and would walk me home. His mother shared that he thought I was his big brother. I felt protective of him.

I was gathering my family to go on a road trip. We planned to find the best roadside autumn displays of flowers to pick and dry. I stepped into the house to grab the picnic basket and when I reappeared he was standing by the car, his doe eyes frightened, looking for security. I violated the rules of my profession and asked if he wanted to join us. My children were under five, and he played with and teased them, communicating child to child. When we stopped for flowers, he would rush ahead and reap large handfuls of fall blossoms. He was a happy child lost in his play and secure in the moment.

He didn't appear for his appointment the following week. His mother called. Carl had befriended neighborhood children. The police had been informed of some inappropriate touch. Carl was deeply shamed and buried in fear. Later that day he disappeared. For three days his family and the community frantically searched for him. Reports came in of a childlike man being seen everywhere. Some fish were stolen off a stringer, and the hope was Carl was hungry and would be coming home soon.

A wind blew cold and the trees began giving up their leaves. The gold and red drapes of fall fell from their limbs. A man taking a break to enjoy his first cigarette of the day spotted Carl. Carl was a religious man. Carl waved in the wind. The man had to adjust his eyes and his brain. Focused, he realized that Carl hung from a high branch, his lifeless body swinging in the cool autumn breeze. Carl was lowered to the ground. He had paid for his sins before dying. He had pounded large nails, spikes, into a board and then pounded the shame-bearing board into his side before stepping off the limb. At the base of the tree lay a bouquet of wildflowers, golden yellows, sky blues, and Lenten purples.

His Death Not A Whisper Stirred

THERE WILL BE no obituary. A few tears may fall. The ground won't shake nor the heavens quake. He may be missed for a minute and a moment. What won't be talked about is the great laughter he brought to this world. No one will discuss the great horror and pain he endured. Will anyone remember the great resolve he showed and the strength he summoned to live his life of humility and love?

Michael's life was lived in jerks and sputters. He started out the bastard child of a street worker. He and an older brother survived long minutes, hours, and years of neglect. Michael forgave his mom. "You know she was mentally ill. She did the best she could?"

Michael was adopted at age six by a professional couple. They each had M.D. on their stationery heading. I grew up with five brothers, so I learned to eat fast if I wanted seconds. Michael was into thirds before I could complete an initial helping. I asked why he ate so fast. He said his parents were embarrassed by him, so when he wasn't in school, he had to stay in his room. He was allowed to eat at the dining table alone. A timer was set for ten minutes and then he was shuttled back to his solitude. His adoptive mom was a singular abuser; she just physically hurt him. His father showed greater contempt and added sexual abuse to the physical harm. Before he was ten Michael had set the house and his school on fire.

He ran away from home at fourteen and lived on the streets of Portland. To survive he sold sex and traded drugs. Juvenile court brought him to the attention of a public prosecutor who turned Michael into his dealer and snitch. Michael didn't know any longer if the voices in his head were his thoughts or demons. Word on the street was that he was a dead man walking.

Somewhere in the insanity of his youth, an older woman saw wounds and wanted to heal the boy. Michael would call her "Grandma." She came to Michael on a winter's day burdened by the rain and snow. She gave him a bus ticket and handed a note to the bus driver. To save his life she put him on a ride to the end of the road. He got off the bus in Ely, Minnesota.

Michael wasn't educated, but he had street savvy. He went to a church and asked for help. The minister, his wife, and their children became the first people he adopted into his new family. He became a community character. He knew everyone, and everyone knew him. He couldn't stop talking. He was laughter and goodwill looking for a chance to be liked.

He pushed his way into my life at a Drop In. He was a poster boy for ADHD, and his brain worked at the speed of bipolar extreme. The only thing that could keep up with his thoughts were his words. He was a talking machine.

I took Michael and a group of folks to the Black Hills. We camped in the mountains. The only sound was the chirping of Michael's voice. He needed to climb the highest peak in those sacred mountains. He was relentless. "Why. Why. Why not. How come. Come on." I broke. Another staff person took Michael to the foot of Mt. Hearny and turned him loose. What could go wrong. There was only one way up and one way down. Michael found another way down. When neither Michael nor the staff person had returned to camp by dark, I began pacing. I walked through the night with the temperature at freezing and the wind toppling trees. My coworker was trapped on the mountain huddled between rocks, hoping to survive to morning. Michael returned to camp at dawn, smiling, laughing, and satiated with buttermilk pancakes. He had taken a wrong turn and found himself at a ranger's home and settled in for a warm night and hot breakfast.

That was Michael.

There was another Michael. This Michael always sold three-quarters of all the tickets of any fund-raiser. He could talk his way into anyone's billfold. His billfold was always empty because he was a sucker for sad tales. He just had to give it all away.

He was a great advocate for the mentally ill. I got a call from him one evening. He had met two young women at a concession stand at a Twins game. He told them of his mission to help people with mental illness. They were consumed by his passion and introduced him to people who introduced him to people, and by the ninth inning he was in the owner's box getting a substantial donation for a new mental health center that was only on the drawing board of other people's minds.

He was a champion bell ringer for the Salvation Army. He was featured in their national magazine. His smile and enthusiastic banter were infectious. The money he earned he used to buy presents for others.

He traveled to New Orleans in the winter to assist the poor in rebuilding their homes. I was never sure if he liked the selfless labor, the southern warmth, or the cheap cigarettes.

Twice I found him overdosed and near death. He quit all the junk and loved the lord. He would call me several times a week to tell me I hadn't called him. I would jokingly tell him I was treating his attachment issues by ignoring his pleas. He'd say "Yeah, but you haven't talked to me for two days. Aren't you my friend? Don't you like me?"

Michael died last night. Alone. Yeah, he was my friend.

Comin' Down in '73

WALKING THE HALL, I was scratching deep and yawning wide. Another long Saturday night of beer. I was on the trail of breakfast. Father John was cooking a gourmet treat as he did every Sunday morning. This would be the last as I was graduating in a week. I walked into his room, my hand still in my underpants. I nodded to the early risers and found a place to hang. Father was his chirpy self and we were all deep in conversations about the future. "I climbed a mountain when I graduated from high school, so maybe I'll just do the same now." Father jumped in. "Take me along." Now I was half awake and talkin' shit, but I was trapped. "All right," and we set a date.

Back in my room several guys stopped to question my judgment. "He's gay. What the hell is wrong with you." Same response to all. "I'm straight and he knows it. Can't we be friends?"

I picked up Father on the designated date, and we headed west. Father had been sober for one year. He had lost his parish call due to his alcoholism and had been teaching English at St. John's. He was a good conversationalist. His chatter and the top forty radio made time pass quickly.

We got into South Dakota when things started getting strange. We drove into a small town just off the freeway for gas and a stretch of the legs. As we pulled into the main street, we found it was shut off with barriers. The only gas station was on the main drag, so I pulled around the barricades and drove to the store. The street was deserted. We filled up and pulled out when we saw movie cameras. We almost made it into a film.

We got to Colorado on the second day and found a campsite close to Long's Peak, the tallest mountain in the state. We set up camp, had dinner, and I wandered off for a walk. The campgrounds were full of co-eds from Colorado schools celebrating the end of the school year. Shared some beers, turned down some tempting offers, and returned to the camp. Father was in the tent. He unzipped the flaps and offered he had a two-man sleeping bag. I begged off and threw my bag near the fire. I was feeling a little uneasy but was sure he had gotten the message.

We broke camp while it was still dark, and the rest of the campgrounds were still sleeping it off. I wanted to get to the trailhead before dawn. The first day's hike to the base of the mountain was going to be strenuous. We packed everything into two packs.

I had Father take the lead. We hadn't walked a half hour when Father was ready to quit. He was in his forties and hadn't prepared in any way for an ascent. I took from his pack the essentials I would need and told him I'd see him in two days. We shook hands, I gave him the keys to my car, and I turned upward; he descended.

I got to the base camp mid-afternoon. It was a large meadow filled with rock. Tent sites had been prepared by moving the largest rocks. I set up camp and sat back with a cup of coffee and some granola. There were six other climbing groups present. Just before dark two young guys set camp. They wandered over for coffee. They were high school grads from Pennsylvania and had come to the mountains on a whim. They were good company and we agreed to climb together.

Before dawn we were on the trail. We were the last group to break camp. It was two hours before we got to the steepest part of the climb. A cable had been cobbled into the mountain to help with the ascent. At the top we rested. The Penn guys weren't doing well. One boy had a serious headache and the other felt nauseous. We sat and rested. Neither got any better. The altitude was punching them in the guts. They turned back.

It took another hour to get to the Key Hole. This rock formation marked the turn of the trail to the backside of the mountain. I caught up with a group of three as they were traversing an ice and snow field. They were using small axes to grip the mountainside. It was straight down 12,000 feet with a single slip. I wasn't so prepared. I followed their tracks. I could look down on other mountaintops and the clouds. Man, it was like being next to God. I used the exhilaration and adrenaline to traverse the ice successfully.

I was near the end of the ascent. The last few hundred feet were straight up over a rugged rock outcropping. I pulled myself over the rim of a rock and I was on the peak. Others were celebrating their ascent with hugs, cheers, and photographs. I sat back against a flat rock and wrote an ode to a recent love. I put it under a large round stone and then rested. In minutes the weather changed. Dark, ominous clouds were rushing in with gusts of wind, and I had to steady myself. The hair of several climbers stood straight up in the static electricity of the storm. A park ranger suddenly appeared and ordered everyone down. I was off the ice when hail and rain began to fall. The wind was to my back and pushed the descent. I got to my tent, changed clothes, and decided I was too tired and cold to eat. I crawled into my bag and shivered through the night.

Morning was a blessing. I delayed heading back to the trailhead and lay on a large flat rock warming in the sun. The hike down was a joy. The sun beamed, and gravity aided the descent. Father John was waiting. He stood next to my car. The front end was smashed and tangled. He was a shallow yellow. Even his eyes had turned. "Jesus Christ, Father, what happened?" His breath fumed alcohol, and when he shifted his weight, he staggered. "Shit, John!"

I angrily threw my pack into the trunk, ordered John into the car, and headed home. It was an uncomfortable ride as he alternately cried and slept. He still had a bottle. When he nodded off, I threw it out.

When we arrived in Grand Island, Nebraska, I was exhausted. I broke the silence to tell John I couldn't go on without some sleep, so he was going to pay for a motel room. We pulled into a mom-and-pop joint. At the desk a grizzled old man told me he had only one room available. It had only a double bed. "Shit," my brain overstated. Exhausted I took the room. I dropped John off and went into town for some meat and bread to make sandwiches. Back at the motel I parked in front of the room. John sat behind the screen door completely naked, his legs spread. "What the f..., John."

"I showered. Just drying myself off."

I pushed past him and put the groceries down. John got out of the chair and dressed. I sat at a small round table unable to hide my anger or discomfort. The TV filled the silence. At dark John went to bed. I rolled my sleeping bag out on the floor. Hours passed, and the floor got harder and John's whimpering became more aggravating.

Sore and deeply exhausted, I told John I needed to

sleep. I threw my bag onto the bed and crawled into it. I hung to the edge of the bed as if my life depended on it. A sneeze would have toppled me. I fell into a fitful sleep. I was awakened to feel John's hand moving up my leg. My arm lay on my hip. When his hand touched mine, I made a fist and sat up. He burst into tears. Great heavy sobs. "Goddamn it, John. Let's go."

I don't remember the trip from Nebraska to the Johnnie campus. It was too long and couldn't end soon enough. I drove up to the monastery. John went in to get help with his gear. I threw it on the lawn and got into the car. As I turned the key, John reemerged bawling like a toddler. I couldn't get away fast enough.

Two weeks later I felt it was all behind me. I couldn't find it in me to ever consider him a friend again. I got a phone call. The voice identified himself as the head of the English department at St. John's.

"John's in treatment, and I was wondering if you could tell me what happened on your trip?"

"It's none of your business."

"I know, but this happens every year. John goes on a trip with someone, and if he scores, he drinks to kill his guilt and remorse, and if he doesn't, he drinks. I just want to know what happened."

I was stunned. "I said it's none of your business." I hung up on faith and friendship.

Questions

I HADN'T FINISHED my first cup of morning coffee when I had to sit in judgment of two throwaways. You know the kind. Clothes worn a few days too long. Haircuts given with home shears. Thin like rails. They walked in slowly, stiffly. They looked at the floor; they looked at each other, then back at the floor. I had my office set up with a desk the size of an aircraft carrier and a chair that did a reasonable impersonation of a throne. When some tough sociopathic son of a bitch walked in, I sat behind my fortress and talked down, establishing who was king. When they seemed frightened, contrite, or out of place, I would come around my desk and sit with them. I sat with these boys.

Their terrible deed was some nonsensical vandalism. My job was to scare them for the courts and offer some community service as restitution for their miscreant behavior. I lightened the mood with some simple conversation, throwing out a line or two of humor, hoping to disarm their fear. They relaxed and

PLAYING COPS

we got on fine. I always told people I got paid to talk shit with teenagers. They were pre-teen, eleven or maybe twelve. They didn't like school, they didn't like authority, and they hated their life situations. They'd been dealt a bad hand. White trash, you know the kind. We joke about the trailer parks, not so cool or hip clothing, bound to become cigarette-smoking, toothless adults. Not knowing them or their situation, we would then call them lazy or welfare cheats. Either way we wouldn't sit near them in a theatre or restaurant. Who'd want to catch whatever it was they had.

But they were kids, so I engaged them. We were laughing about stupid shit, when one of them threw out a slang term I had never heard before. They both began laughing outrageously. I asked what the hell they were talking about. In between gasps of breath they explained that it meant if you bent over in the shower, Mr. H was going to give you the hot hard one in the butt. They kept laughing, entertained that they could talk to an adult like he was just one of them. Now this was the early eighties, and as a culture we were just beginning to understand again how common the sexual abuse of children was. I had just been to some training with a Chicago reporter who thought sexual abuse of kids was more the national pastime than baseball.

I asked for an explanation and they picked up on my seriousness. They became somber and began squirming again. Silence didn't just fall like a curtain;

QUESTIONS

it came down like a death shroud. The next half hour was torturous. They talked about how "other kids" were being sexually molested in their town and that it was so common, it had become part of the lexicon of all the troubled boys in the community. I assumed they were talking about themselves, but this was not the time for pressuring them into remembering events that most likely would haunt them the rest of their lives.

When they left, I went and shared what I heard and what I suspected with my partner, Pat. She was diminutive in stature but was passionate as hell about kids. She had coal-black hair and a darker complexion. Her surname was Irish and she joked she was Black Irish, a noun for Irish of Spanish descent. We took the story to the Social Services department. The social worker was stunned. What we were all trying to understand seemed improbable. These two waifs were claiming that the mayor of the next community, a professional businessman of considerable influence, a man who had developed a neighborhood in the community, naming streets after his children, was an ogre, a destroyer of children.

Social services should have been the investigators; they were experienced but scared of the possible political fallout. Pat and I were new to corrections and young enough to still charge at dragons. We got the name of a mental health professional who specialized in interviewing children who were suspected of having been abused. His name was Tom. He shared within the first five minutes of meeting us that he had been abused and he was now on a mission to ferret out perverts wherever they lived. He was jumpy and nervous and he would charge up every environment we entered.

A week after the initial interviews with our first potential victims, we found ourselves in the enemy's hometown. We had been offered an office in the Catholic rectory, which was close to the public school. Arrangements had been made to interview the young boys who had initially garnered our concerns. They went into the room with Tom together. Pat and I waited in the hall. We wandered around looking at papers posted on the walls, trying to seem interested in the old black-and-white photos of long-departed priests. Tom burst out of the office yelling in a whisper, "We got the bastard." Pat and I stood in silence waiting for our brains to understand the magnitude of what was just said. "We got the bastard." The boys left with their parents and were told we'd be getting into contact with them.

Tom was energized. He paced the hallway as we scuttled along behind him. Both boys told similar stories. They had met Mr. H, who was a veterinarian. He befriended them, and they hung around his office, getting to play with animals kept overnight. He was nice and gave them lots of attention. He bought them things and then they got to go with him into the country to see the farm animals the doc worked on. When trust was established, Doc would pull over in a secluded wooded spot and pull out a six-inch syringe and inform the boys they had to now perform favors for him, or the large needle was going to hurt like hell.

Tom spun around. "There's more victims; go find them." He must have seen the dumb look on my face. He slowed his pace and talked in a normal tone and rate of speed. "Go to the school yard, and when you see a boy who resembles our two victims, bring him here." I was known at the school, so I spoke with the principal. During the lunch period, Pat and I stood in the recess area and pointed at young boys who met the classification we were looking for, "throwaways."

One by one Tom interviewed four more boys. They all shared the same story. Our exhilaration on discovering the first victims turned to sorrow. The charge of excitement wasn't the same each time Tom emerged from an interview to share we had found another. Pain brings an awkward silence. Pat and I could only share a short moment of grief each time. We knew a great storm was brewing.

In a state of shock, we agreed to meet Tom at a local coffee hangout to discuss strategy and decompress. As we talked I wondered how many more boys there could be. Locals came in and out of the restaurant. We remained huddled in a corner talking in hushed tones. I sat back and took a sip of coffee, feeling heartburn. I turned toward the counter and saw the local deputy sheriff standing there. I tried to look away, but he had met my gaze and came to our table. He was a hopeless dufus. We entertained him with small talk. He finally asked why we were in town. I motioned him to lean forward and asked for his silence in what I was about to share. I unfolded the story. He caught his breath and began to laugh. "Everybody knows that. Hell, my buddies and I scared each other with those stories when I was in school." I looked at him in bewilderment. He couldn't shut up. "I know some guys our age," meaning early thirties, "who were raped by him." I walked down the block to a business to talk to the owner whom the deputy had indicated had been hurt by Mr. H, nearly twenty years before. The store owner wasn't stunned; he seemed relieved to share his story. Now we had victims age twelve to thirty-two. I drove home that Friday wondering how someone's heart could be devoid of compassion. Not just someone—it was beginning to appear a whole community had lost its soul.

I returned to work the following Monday with a notice to go see the judge. I knocked and entered his chambers. I knew he was upset. He was twirling a curl of hair in the middle of his forehead and he had spittle building in the left corner of his mouth, which held his cigar. He cut to the chase immediately. He didn't like that I had been part of the investigative team. He argued I was a representative of the court and I couldn't show any bias. I argued I had responsibility for the kids on my caseload. He turned from his usual bourbon blush to a strawberry red. He didn't like it when I disagreed. He sent me home to think. It was four days later when he allowed me to return to work. This was to become a tradition. I would disagree with him, and home I'd go until I could show appropriate contrition. Two stubborn Micks unable to see the value of a healthy relationship.

Three weeks later charges were brought and Mr. H was arrested. He was immediately bailed out. I was worried about the kids. How would they react to the knowledge of their rapist being released without any hesitation? That should have been the least of my worries. When word spread through the community that an upstanding citizen like Mr. H had been arrested due to the testimony of riffraff, the good people became outraged. A church service was held with Mr. H in attendance so that he could receive the prayers and support of the congregation. I checked on my boys. The original two had been identified as the rats. They had been unmercifully harassed by classmates. One of the victims was so frustrated he slammed his hand into a wall and was now wearing a cast. I tried to help them see that this would blow over. I tried to comfort them with the understanding they were the victims and Mr. H the villain. One man's word doesn't stand up to a village. They were completely demoralized. They cried and threatened suicide. For their courage, they were driven to madness.

Two weeks later Mr. H had his first appearance in court scheduled. He was to appear on a Monday afternoon. I spent the Saturday before lost in worry. How would the young male victims withstand the onslaught of press once the court proceedings started? It never got that far.

Mr. H went mad. He went to his office armed with a shotgun, called his wife and special friends, and declared suicidal intent. When those who loved and cherished him most were at his door, pounding and crying out in their pain, he stood behind the door and pulled the trigger. His victims would not have their day in court, and the community would always be left with the doubt of his guilt.

A week later I received a phone call from the sheriff. Mr. H's brother was at the office and would like to talk to me. I felt I was walking into a trap. I was convinced he felt that I had conspired with some raggedy youths to drive his brother to suicide. He was in mourning. His eyes were red from tears. He asked politely for what I knew of the case. I explained as best I could without details. He seemed to understand. He spoke with sadness and defeat. "You need to understand my brother wasn't a bad person. We grew up on a farm, and my dad would hire transient men to help with the harvests. When my brother was twelve, he was sexually assaulted by one of the laborers."

I felt his pain and I understood his brother's pain. I still question, however: how do you put compassion into a man's heart? How do you get a village to raise all their children?

Daydreams, musings, and other delusions
A Little Fiction

The Christmas IOU

"SARA. SARA!"

The little girl looked up, but only for a moment. Her eyes quickly darted down to the letter she was writing in red and green crayon. "Dear Santa," it began.

"Sara," the woman said with some pleasantry still in her voice. "Sara, you are my Christmas child. Your hair is as red as Rudolph's nose, and your skin is as white and soft as the snow." She was proud of herself for finishing the sentence without slurring a word. She stood up, whirled toward the kitchen, and decided to reward herself with some Christmas punch.

Sara paid no attention. Her tongue darted out of the right corner of her mouth as she tried to find the perfect words for her letter. She switched to the green crayon, and in the best cursive any nine-year-old had ever written, she continued.

Dear Santa,

I don't want much for myself Santa, but my puppy Ralph needs a bed. Can you find one that is soft and warm. Ralph loves to cuddle. My brother Joey would like a pair of jeans. He'd really like a pair that no one else has ever worn. I'm not going to ask for myself because I know you will bring me the perfect gift. Just not moon boots again. I will have cookies for you.

Love ooxx,
Sara

She carefully folded it twice and put it in her pocket. She thought she heard glass breaking, so she stood up and hurried to the kitchen. Ralph stood over her mom. The slight woman lay in a small pool of blood. She had dropped the bottle of whiskey and cut her hand. Sara helped her sit up. She pulled her mother's hair back, stroking it, assuring her that she was okay. She got a wet cloth and wrapped her mom's bloody hand in it.

"I tripped over that damn dog."

Sara wanted to say, "No you didn't—you're drunk," but she knew all too well her mother would not hear her. Instead she gave Ralph a hug and let him outside. "Stay in the yard; it's cold today." Turning back to her mother, she helped her to her feet. She took her hand and led her to the kitchen table and had her sit down. Her mother lay her head on her arms and began to gently sob herself to sleep. Sara sat for a moment, and when she was sure that her mother was asleep, she let Ralph back in. She and Ralph went to the front room to watch TV. They sat next to each other on the couch. Ralph first lay his head on her shoulder, then slid down, laying his head in her lap. Sara absentmindedly petted his neck and played with his ear. It was a moment of peace in a world yet to explode.

Sara was lost in her head when Joey threw himself down next to her. "What's up, sis."

Sara put a finger to her lips and shushed Joey. "Mom's sleeping."

"You know she's drunk. Why don't you just admit it?" Joey was impatient with Sara. "You're always defending her. Just say it. She's a drunk."

Sara bit her lip and slipped farther down into the cushions. She didn't like these arguments. She knew what her mother was, but Joey refused to see the other parts of her. Her mother could be kind and attentive. She fixed most meals. She tried to keep the house up. She sometimes was awake when Sara went to bed and she'd tuck her in and tell her she was her "special little girl." Sara hardened and wished her brother to leave.

"If she's such a good mom, why aren't there decorations or even a tree in the house? It's Christmas—everyone else has something. What do we got?" He was getting mad. He did what he did when he was angry. He took out a cigarette and went to the porch to smoke. He was only thirteen, but he'd been smoking two years. Sara knew better than to say anything about that dirty habit. As he went out the door, he slammed his fist into the wall. Sara jumped. She knew he was going to hit the wall, but she jumped. She always jumped when the anger started.

It was starting to get dark. Sara felt her muscles tighten. She felt an ache begin in the back of her head. She knew it would work its way around to her forehead, and then it would begin to pound. Her stomach started to churn. She didn't need to look at the clock; it was time for her dad to drive up to the house. Sara went to her room and lay down on her bed. Vertigo took over. Sara got up and went to her safe place. She sat in the back of her closet with her feet against the door. She was holding out all the evil in the world. As his father's car pulled up to the front, Joey was out the back door. His shelter and security were the old barn.

Sara listened. His steps were precise. His cough was raspy but firm. The door opened. "Hey there, Ralph." His words were drunken. Sara let out a long, slow breath. Should she run out and welcome him? She caught herself and decided she'd better wait. She pushed her door open just a crack, pressed herself back against the wall, and held her breath. She heard a faint laugh from her mother. Then her dad laughed. Everyone was safe.

Sara quietly descended the stairs and tiptoed through the house. She entered the kitchen. Her parents were at the table. "Hi," she said and got a drink

THE CHRISTMAS IOU

of water. She went to the back door and waved at the barn. Joey got the okay to come in. Sara put peanut butter on three pieces of bread. Her parents were having their first beer. Sara gave one piece of bread to Ralph. She left one on the bannister for Joey and went back to her room, dinner in hand.

She awoke at dawn. Ralph was sleeping under her bed. She could hear her dad snoring. Her mom was moving in the kitchen. Everyone safe. No fights during the night. It just might be a traditional Christmas Eve. In the beginning the family would have a turkey dinner with all the trimmings, and while the family minus Dad drove around looking at Christmas lights, Santa would come. It was the best feeling in the world to come in from the chilled night and see presents under the warm glow of the Christmas tree.

Sara entered the kitchen, where Mom was making dressing. Sara asked to help, and she put on an apron. She carried things and fetched things, she stirred things and she mixed things. She smiled at her mom and wished things could always be like this.

Joey came into the kitchen and sat on the stool in the corner. He tried to give directions, but Sara and her mother pretended not to hear. Laughter and smiles would bake and cook this meal. They got Joey into an apron, and he started on the sugar cookies. His job was to cut them out, and later they'd all decorate the bells and stars.

Dad got up around noon. He stretched and

yawned as he entered the kitchen. He gave everyone a smile and sat down next to the coffeepot. He had two cups of coffee and was started on a third when he suggested he might put some Christmas cheer into the dark brew. Everyone paused for a moment. Only the radio made a sound. Dad got up, looked through several cupboards, and pulled down a bottle. "Honey, how about a toast to the holiday season." Mom didn't respond. She kept her head down and her hands busy. Dad poured two glasses and set one in front of his wife. "To Santa and all his reindeer. A speedy trip." He tipped the glass back and emptied it. He gently chided his wife as he poured another. She hesitated. Looked at Sara. Joey glared as she took a small sip and set the glass down. Dad was on his fourth; he walked over, handed his wife her glass, and topped it off. "May all your dreams come true." They both drank.

By two o'clock the dinner was in the oven. Mom had lain down for a nap in the corner of the kitchen, a bottle between her splayed legs. Dad had left for town to pick up "a few things." Joey and Sara retreated to their rooms, and Sara prayed that the Ghost of Christmas Past wasn't going to visit again.

It was getting dark when Sara heard her mother moving in the kitchen. She asked Joey if he'd like to go down with her and help Mom with the dinner. He sadly shook his head. He shrugged his shoulders as if to say, "what for?" and lit a cigarette.

Sara went down. The kitchen was warm and

smelled like a feast. "Hey, Mom."

"Hey, yourself. Are you hungry." Mom had cleared the cookie dough from the table and had placed three plates down.

"Where's Dad?"

"Getting things. I don't think we'll wait for him. He'll probably be late. Call your brother."

Mom sat in her usual place: Sara to her left and Joey at her right. They filled their plates and ate with anticipation, all ears leaning toward the front door and the sound of a car returning. Small talk was made. Single bites were filling nervous stomachs.

Ralph felt the tension and moved from his rug in the living room to lie at Sara's feet. She hand-fed him from her plate. Mom went to the counter, picked up the whiskey, and poured a small drink into her coffee cup. She poured the rest down the sink. Dinner was done. Everyone sat in the quiet of the evening. A storm was rising.

Dark had long set in when Dad stumbled through the door. He dropped the presents in his arms when he tripped on the rug. He fell forward, smashing the coffee table. He staggered to his feet and entered the kitchen as Joey was running out the back door. Joey would run to wherever it was he ran to. Mom stiffened. Sara wrapped her arms around Ralph, who was shaking.

He sat down. "Where's my dinner?" It didn't sound hardly like English, but Sara's mom quickly filled a plate and put it in front of her husband. "I can't eat this shit cold." He threw the plate at the wall. Ralph shrunk back from the table. Sara prepared to jump.

"I can warm you a plate," said Sara's mom. She bent forward to pick up the bowl of potatoes when he hit her in the face with his hand. She fell back into her chair stunned. Blood came from her nose and lip. Sara reached to wipe away the blood when he pushed her out of her chair and onto the floor. Ralph started to bark and stood over Sara. Dad picked up the turkey and slammed it into his wife's head. Drippings and grease trickled down into the blood on her face. She rolled over and ran for the stairs. He was behind her. As she scrambled up the stairs, he caught her by her long hair and pulled her over backward, and she fell down the stairs. He lost his balance and landed next to his wife. He rolled and straddled her, hitting her over and over. She covered her face with her arms. Ralph grabbed him by his raised arm and tore a gaping hole in his flesh. He pulled away. Ralph had him by a leg and wouldn't let go. Sara ran for her closet. In the darkness of her sanctuary, she called 911. She sat back and disappeared into her mind.

When she allowed herself to hear again, it was extraordinarily quiet. She listened hard for any noise. Her body was ready to recoil on the smallest signal of danger. Her breath came fast. Her heart was pulsing. She pulled her legs back and opened her door. Nothing. She started down the stairs. One foot and

THE CHRISTMAS IOU

one stair at a time. Between each step she stopped to listen and then she would creep forward one more step.

No one was in the house. There were bandages and coverings on the floor. An EMT bag had been forgotten. Sara felt relief. Ralph came from the kitchen. They sat together for a moment. She noticed the gifts her father had dropped. She gathered them. One had her name. She carefully unwrapped it and opened the small box. A piece of folded paper lay on the bottom. "Sorry, baby, maybe next year. IOU." Ralph gently licked away her falling tears.

Another Suck-Ass Day in Paradise

THE SUN HAD barely cracked the northern sky when the alarm went off. The gray haze of a new morning made it difficult for Jaden to read the clock's hands. He slumped back down and threw a pillow over his face. He exhaled a couple of times when he heard the shrieking of his mother's voice. "Time to get up!" Jaden blocked an inappropriate response and just grunted. He was nearing that neverland between sleep and consciousness when the Shriek, as he called his mother, screamed, "You lazy…get your…out of bed now!" Jaden smiled. It was going to be another suck ass day in paradise.

He pulled on his cleanest pair of dirty jeans and found a T-shirt that didn't smell too bad. As he walked to the bathroom, he lit up a smoke and allowed the calm that always followed to find its way down his lean torso. He stood over the toilet, and as the stream partially found the target, he looked into the mirror with disgust at the face that leered back. He grabbed his coat and skirted out the front door, intentionally avoiding the kitchen and the Shriek. He hadn't had a civil word with her in weeks, and he feared he never would again. She constantly berated his old man, and the comparisons she made between him and his dad sucked big-time. The old man was an a-hole, and Jaden didn't need to hear it. Life is a struggle and then you die, so who needs details.

The walk was six blocks. He was headed toward the Alternative School. It's where all the other perps, dorks, shitheads, and assholes went to school. It was great—no one expected anything, and he gave nothing. By chance a bike lay on the front lawn of a small neat house. He grabbed it and pedaled down to the school. He threw the bike against the wall, bending a tire. *Cheap shit*, he thought. He bounced into the building and immediately changed his mood. The chip on his shoulder expanded, and darkness settled into his eyes. He looked at the floor and followed familiar tiles to the lunch room, where he hoped to score a little breakfast.

The cooks were putting things away, so he quickly grabbed a couple of milks and stuffed them into his coat pockets. Carol, the happy cook, noticed and smiled at him. Jaden pretended not to notice. He grabbed at some toast when Attila the Hun, Jaden's name for the angry cook with the lazy eye, said,

"We're closed. Try to get here on time."

Jaden slipped a couple F-bombs under his breath. Attila read his lips and threatened him with detention. He let a bomb drop as loud as he could scream and threw a milk at her. Seeking sanctuary, he raced for the bathroom, slumped into a stall, and lit up. The smoke was harsh and he started coughing. He struggled not to throw out a lung. A second tug on the cig brought relief. The bathroom door opened and Jaden tensed for a fight. He glared through the crack in the stall and saw dipshit Degan walk to a urinal.

"Hey, dipshit," Jaden called out as he stepped out from his shelter. "Did you see Wandersee anywhere?" Jaden was referencing the principal. He was new but he was marked. A principal is a principal.

"Shit no, why would I want to see him," the dipshit replied.

"He's probably looking for me. I gave Attila some lip, so I'm probably on the ten most wanted list."

Jaden handed the smoke to Degan, who took a deep hit and passed it back.

"Damn, I'm hungry, man." Jaden frowned. "I was out till two last night, and the Shriek ate all the pizza before I got home and then Attila slammed the door on toast. God, I hate them all."

Degan reached into his pocket and pulled out a napkin wrapped around a day-old doughnut. He broke off half and handed it to Jaden. "Gotta run, bro—enjoy."

ANOTHER SUCK-ASS DAY IN PARADISE

Jaden took a bite, spit it out, and threw the mash against the wall. Anger closed his throat and he couldn't swallow. He quickly worked through all his pockets and surprised himself to find a dollar in change. He carefully opened the bathroom and checked the hallway in both directions. He stepped out cautiously and then skulked down the hall to the commons area to get a pop.

He leaned against the machine, deciding which pop would do the job. He was thinking about what a shit-ass day this was turning into. They were all shit-ass days, so he stopped thinking about it and pressed a button. Nothing. He jammed it a couple more times. He slammed his fist into the button. The physical jolt released a vomit of anger that was boiling in his stomach, and he threw himself into destroying the machine. He was fighting for his life.

He brought everything he had into the fight. He kicked and wailed. He threw his shoulders into the stomach of the metal Titan. He pelted it with a succession of full punches, lost in the bloodlust. Only vaguely aware of people standing around, bug-eyed with open mouths, he kept up the assault until exhausted and then he lay prone against the grinning machine. He heard the sound of muffled voices and the patterned taps of shoes quickly leaving the scene. His lungs ached and his head throbbed. He didn't know what to do next. Frustration and anger were crawling up his throat, and he was afraid he was going to cry.

He sucked in a stomach full of air and pulled back, standing straight.

"Mr. Whitehead." Jaden shuddered at the sound of his name. He cautiously looked over his shoulder. A man in a suit stood still, about ten feet away. He stood calmly. His voice didn't challenge. There was no hint of anger. "Jaden, I'm Mr. Wandersee. May I talk to you?"

Jaden braced himself. He tightened his hands into fists as he pivoted to engage in war again. He measured the man. Jaden knew he was in trouble. The man towered over him. His only chance was to find his fury. He lowered his eyes and felt the rumblings of the storm he kept hidden deep in his brain stem. Life or death. He got ready to charge.

"Jaden," the man said. He stood with his arms at his side, his hands open. He showed no fear. Jaden couldn't read him. He stepped back one step, continuing to measure his new enemy. He looked again at the floor.

"Jaden, may I speak to you?" Wandersee didn't move. He cracked a strange little smile. "That machine likes to steal my money too. Maybe I should give it a couple of good whacks." Jaden kept his head down but he looked up, puzzled.

"Jaden, can we talk?"

Jaden shuffled his feet and awkwardly blurted, "Yeah."

"I heard there was an accident in the lunch room.

Some milk was spilled. I was wondering if I could get your help in cleaning it up."

Jaden struggled to understand. Alarms were screaming inside his head, but he couldn't detect the threat. His body wanted to run and his brain was screaming with fear.

Wandersee silently stood for a few seconds. Jaden felt the tension in his muscles slowly withdraw. He opened his hands and stretched his fingers, which ached. "What?" was all he could muster.

"I've got this new suit, so I was wondering if I could get your help with cleaning up some milk that was spilled in the dining hall. It won't take long." Wandersee turned ninety degrees, as if he was leaving.

Jaden was struggling to find the angle. What was the scam? Where did the trick lie? He took two cautious steps toward Wandersee. The man put out his hand. Jaden took it, not knowing what to expect. The man shook it firmly and smiled as he released it.

"I appreciate you helping me, Jaden. I was having a tough day. It's nice to get some cooperation." They started down the hall in lockstep. Wandersee kept talking. "The cooks told me they noticed a problem today. They think maybe they need to loosen up on hours. They told me that they can't be too strict on time. They've been noticing some kids get to school late and come hungry. They asked if they could keep food handy all day just for snacks. I told them, they're in charge, it's their kitchen." Wandersee halted. Jaden stiffened.

Wandersee reached into his pocket and Jaden felt fear. Wandersee's hand came out. He offered Jaden a dollar bill. "Here, in the future, when that machine screws with you, just come and find me."

They continued down the hall. Jaden felt a little lighter. His head didn't hurt so much.

Falling for Love

> Narcolepsy: a chronic sleep disorder characterized by excessive sleepiness and sleep attacks at inappropriate times.
>
> Cataplexy: a sudden muscular weakness brought on by strong emotions.

WHEN ALEX WAS sixteen, he fell face first in love. He was hanging with his comrades in the school hallway making like Olympic judges as they graded the sway in the hips of the young coeds. The flow of her skirt came around the corner first. Then the fresh splash of her shoulder-length hair cascaded into full view, and she flowed into his mind. Alex was mesmerized by the sparkle in her eyes. He quickly moved his eyes from her dimples to her ankles, and that's when he began to feel those first strange tinglings of love. His heart started a strange patterned rhythm, and his throat started to close. He focused on her pouting lips and felt weak-kneed. At arm's length he was overwhelmed with the essence of flowers and honey. He closed his eyes to fully engage the scent and fell headlong into love. He first leaned into her, bouncing off her chest; he then pivoted and fell head first into the floor, breaking his nose and lying in utter disgrace.

His buddies broke out with stomach-aching laughter. It was Alex's best stunt yet. She screamed as if assaulted and actually raised her hand for a good slap, but Alex was already on his way down, so she stopped herself and then stepped over his prone body, making sure her heel pinched some of his forearm skin to the floor. Feeling satisfied she strutted on.

Finally someone noticed a little trickle of blood, and that Alex lay like a felled tree, his limbs splayed, hadn't moved. In fact he had the peaceful look of someone sound asleep, and he was. *Alex had a big stiffy* became the grinding, unnerving singsong that would follow Alex throughout high school. He was doomed.

The first attack was thought to be low sugar. When it happened again everyone thought maybe Alex had a social anxiety problem or maybe a specific phobia to girls. His buddies of course thought it was caused by the arousal of certain body parts and that Alex wasn't man enough to hold his up. Eventually the total number of episodes started to outweigh any individual possible causation. Alex was taking dives whenever he felt happiness or excitement of any kind. He certainly didn't share how he had never successfully stimulated himself. Hidden under his covers, working devilishly fast so no one interrupted, he would be reaching for the peak and...then he'd be awakened by his own snoring and a drivel of spit in the corner of his mouth. No pleasure ever known.

Adolescence was not only confusing for Alex, it was escaping his grasp. There was no sex, no rock and roll. If he let the music take him or if he allowed a sexual twinge to any fantasy, he would awaken following a high dive from an emotional platform. He was lucky to escape these episodes without cuts and bruises. He had found himself on classroom floors, lying sprawled across neighbors' lawns, and once he awoke to find his face enmeshed in the mash potatoes, with gravy on his lap.

He discovered that if he didn't feel, if he didn't have an emotional response, he could navigate the day without incident. He spent hours practicing his "stone face." He would lie on his bed and repeat to himself over and over jokes that had caused laughter, until he felt no response. He would envision the faces of girls he dreamed of meeting. He'd focus his thoughts and shut down all emotional responses. He taught himself to be void of joy, excitement, anger, and love.

His friends were more than willing to test his resolve. They'd set up elaborate pranks to tease and frustrate him. Once he rounded the hall corner leaving math class, and his best two buddies were bent over, pants to their ankles and butt cheeks exposed. Alex looked straight ahead, bit his lip to feel pain, and walked away.

Alex avoided anything that was too stimulating. He stopped going to movies. Action pictures elevated his testosterone, and in the excitement he'd spill his drink and popcorn and awaken looking at the blankness of the floor. Comedies found him splayed on the floor like a fileted mackerel. Love stories had him swooning and falling. Alex found that all the wonderful experiences of adolescence were to be held at a distance. He stopped listening to music, gave up TV, and stayed away from athletic events and group outings. He became a statue, bound up in the cement of indifference. But he missed one thing. He needed one thing. He had to have love.

Alex became a science experiment. He was prescribed drugs of different colors and different shapes. He would take them in different amounts and different combinations, looking for the key that would allow him to participate in life. The doctors found a combination that froze most of his feelings, and Alex didn't have to walk on pins and needles, waiting for the next emotional burst that would flatten him. With meds and a stoic lack of passion, he slipped through the days. But he always wondered about love.

In his senior year he sat next to Annakiesha in two

FALLING FOR LOVE

classes. She had the complexion of milk chocolate. Her eyes beamed life and enticement, and her hair bounced to the rhythms of joy and happiness. He felt something.

From the first day he had noticed her, he formulated a plan to meet her without any acrobatics. He had to be more than a robot. Her mere presence would send a warm flush through his torso. He would begin yawning and knew this was a sign of danger. You can't profess great love while napping. As soon as he noticed any flush feelings, he'd pinch himself, until his brain screamed enough.

Every night he would chant her name, Annakiesha, Annakiesha, Annakiesha. He would envision her smile and as he felt the emotional attachments rise, he would combat them with a counting system to temper the rising interest and excitement. He learned to effectively modulate his feelings. Everything became regulated.

After several weeks of desensitizing himself to all imagined emotional response, he felt ready to proceed. He could call her name, he could imagine her embrace, he could envelop her scent as she sat next to him, and he only needed to stifle the smallest of yawns.

On a Tuesday morning he got to class early. He felt an impulse of excitement and bit his inner lip. He took out a sheet of paper, tore it in half, and in a stilted and very pragmatic hand wrote. "My name is Alex.

May I talk to you some time?" He took two great gulps of air to steady himself and waited for the right moment in class. When he felt no one was watching, he scanned his body for any sign of tension and reached across the aisle with the note in his hand.

He awoke fifteen minutes later. The room was empty. Everyone had moved on to the next class. He muffled another yawn, rubbed his eyes, and then remembered the note. He looked about. It had disappeared. A tweak of anxiety began to rise. What if the teacher took the note? God forbid his buddies had it in hand. He leaned back in his chair; alternately making fists and releasing the tension, he fought to dispel the anxious feelings. He picked up his books and walked steadily to his next class.

Alex kept a stress ball in his jacket pocket. When he sat in class the following day, he worked it like a dog on a new bone. Annakiesha entered and smiled. He felt his temperature spike. She flashed a shy smile in his direction and looked to the floor. He felt a little warmth in his groin area, moving up to his stomach. As she took her seat, she opened her hand and showed him the note and nodded yes. He awoke within ten minutes.

They communicated by note for several weeks. His stilted and controlled. Her notes were of the typical teen interests. What music do you listen to, who's

FALLING FOR LOVE

your favorite actor, movies you've seen, and do you really like me? To the last question, he wrote...Y...e... and it was nap time.

Two weeks later they had arranged to meet. He had asked to walk her home. They met at her locker. "Hi," she said. He nodded. It wasn't even a cool nod, just a mechanical "how do you do." They turned toward the doors and began their walk. He reached to open the door for her, and his hand touched hers.

He awoke slouched against the wall. His eyes were down, focused on his shoes. He gently shook his head to refresh himself and he remembered her. He looked slowly up to an empty hallway and then turned to his left. She sat silently next to him, his books gathered into her arms. "Good morning." She giggled.

Each afternoon they would start their walk, and each afternoon they ventured a little nearer to their goal. They would devise little strategies to stretch out each walk. Some days, feeling a little devilish, Annakiesha would intentionally brush her hand ever so gently against his. She would laugh softly as he would straighten, yawn, and then gently and slowly crumple to the ground, falling into a puddle of melted emotions. She thought of it as a love meter. Alex would never be able to hide his true feelings from her.

It took three months for the couple to work up to the first real date. Alex walked to Annakiesha's home. He rang the doorbell and felt his jaw slacken, so he snapped his head back and thought of a math formula. He regained his steadiness as the door opened. They walked to the school side by side. She, bouncing and flirting, an adolescent caught up in the joys and entangled feelings of early romance, and he ramrod straight, devoid of facial expression but burning with buried love.

She loved to dance. She was like a bird in the wind. She gracefully moved within the moment of the beat. She whirled and twirled in the rhythm of love. Alex purposefully balanced from one foot to the next, rocking like a broken hobby horse. He kept the beat but appeared as a rigid, plastic toy soldier incapable of more than one pose. Together they projected a picture of an unencumbered fairy playfully darting about a silent tree. But they were together and it was working.

They had a wonderful evening. They left the dance with Alex containing his passion, but they walked hand in hand. They came to a home with a retaining wall just waist high where they sat, still hand in hand. Alex softly squeezed Annakiesha's hand with his left hand while he furiously squeezed the stress ball with his right. She leaned into him and ever so gently kissed his lips. The tightness in his body dissipated; he went flush and his body turned to putty. He slowly fell back into sweet dreams.

He awakened from a dream of butterflies to the gentle fluttering of Annakeisha's eyelashes against his cheek. He melted again. He awakened again and again, and she would smile, squeeze his hand, and softly stroke his cheek or alternately run her fingers through his hair, and he would relapse into dreams of kites, birds, and lovely days.

He awoke to see her face framed by the stars of a sparkling night. She stepped back and helped him to his feet. Hand in hand they finished the walk to her home. At the door he braced himself for one last kiss. He began running geometry formulas through his brain as he kissed her long and slowly, bracing himself against love. She quietly pulled away, smiled, and disappeared into her home. He stood on her doorstep. He straightened himself and began to recite "The Rime of the Ancient Mariner." Before he could turn away, he allowed himself to feel again the sweetness of her mouth, and he slipped to the ground. He slept at her door, a boy of many complicated feelings, totally in love.

Family Transgressions

MATT JOHNSON WAS a man of determination. He was a man of righteousness. He pulled his chair square so he could command a view of the road and see vehicles approaching from either direction. He pulled a blanket up around his shoulders, placed the shotgun across his lap, and waited.

Matt had faced his final humiliation. That morning he had been released from jail, and he came home to a vacant house. Everything had been picked up and everything was in its place. At least she had gotten that right. Matt seethed with anger. He gritted his teeth and massaged his right temple as he reconsidered everyone's action that prior Thanksgiving. She had insisted on having her family over. He was against it, but he had allowed his charitable side to override his rational mind. A mistake he rarely made. He kicked the chair leg with his heel in disgust. He had been weak again, and see what it got him? He looked at the shotgun and rubbed the wood grain. It was a thing of beauty. She would learn her lesson this time.

He shifted his weight in the chair. A red pickup came down the road. He recognized it as his neighbor Ed's; Ed was probably coming home from work. He'd known Ed for fifteen years, and they had maybe spoken five times. People should just attend to their own business was Matt's way of thinking. Ed waved and Matt nodded. He didn't want the fool to stop. There was no time for insipid conversation. Ed drove past and Matt sighed with relief, placing his right hand on the cold steel barrel.

"Son of a bitch!" Matt chastised himself. Why had he allowed himself to be conned into sitting down to dinner with a table full of people he detested. "Oh, it will be great to see the grandkids," she had whined, and he had bought it. They weren't his grandkids, especially the darker ones. "Indian, bullshit—they were black, didn't matter what continent their people came from. Dot, not feather," he chuckled to himself.

He pulled the blanket tighter and a little shiver went from his back down his arms. Hadn't he welcomed them into his home? Hadn't he offered them his food? They came into the house with their platitudes and fake smiles. He'd been such a sucker. She probably planned it all. She knew it was going to end badly. "Shit," he said aloud. He would bet they all had it planned. All those years of taking care of her, going the extra mile to daily take her to work and pick her up. He had to do everything to make sure they had worked as a couple. He managed the money, made the decisions about who they would see and where they would go. She was too stupid to do any of that. She had forced him to this point. She had set this all up. She was going to pay for all those years of deceit and contrariness.

A dog barked somewhere out in the woods. Matt's lips parted in a grin of recognition that someone else was on the hunt. It was totally dark now; only the stars shed any light. Matt just knew she would sneak back in the night to get her stuff. That's how they all were, especially the dark ones, sneaky.

"Thanksgiving, for Christ's sake." What was there to be thankful for? Dinner had started out fine. Small talk and hadn't he been gracious. He sat at the head as usual and led grace. He had carved the turkey. They were thankless ingrates. Dinner would have passed peacefully except he, the dark one, asked how work was. "Screw him," Matt congratulated himself. He knew Matt had been laid off just days before. He asked the question like he knew something. He was laying the bait. She probably had told him to bring it up, to expose to the family Matt's sins. It wasn't his fault he was out of work. They knew he was laid off because the store was failing. His smile gave him away. He wanted to shame Matt. "Screw them." Matt stomped his feet and blew hot breath into his cupped hands, flexed his fingers, and returned them to the gun.

Headlights appeared. Matt slid his right index

finger onto the trigger. The car didn't slow and Matt didn't recognize the vehicle. "They'll be here and they won't be leaving again."

Matt replayed the dinner over and over in his mind. He had put that smart-ass in his place. He had replaced that son of a bitch's smirk with the fear of god. Then she had stood up. He didn't give her a chance to interfere. He pushed her aside to get to the turban head. She stumbled. She was accident prone. She fell and her chair tipped with her. Then they all went nuts. Rushing about, yelling like the mad asses they were. He cursed them good. He hit one of his stepdaughters with the potato bowl. One of the dark-skinned grandkids was knocked to the floor with the turkey plate. "No one disrespects me in my home," Matt had shouted. They knew he had a temper, but they baited him. They knew what they were doing and they got exactly what they deserved.

Matt had begun to clean up the mess when the cops showed up. "Never in my life have I been arrested. It was family business. They called the cops and they'll pay," he said to himself over and over. That's when the final plan began to formulate. He spent two days in jail. He had been humiliated, placed in cuffs, photographed, and fingerprinted like a common crook. There was hell to be paid. She instigated it. She would answer for it.

Matt began to feel more chilled. He shivered again and pulled the blanket tighter and zipped his coat. She would be coming. She would use the dark to cover her deceptions, but he was ready. The stars sparkled brightly and a new moon sat high in the sky. Coyotes howled a chorus to the north. The pack was celebrating the kill. Matt howled back. The kill was all-important.

The chill of the night was passing. Matt had fought the tiredness that crept in, but he slowly sank into a troubled slumber. Even asleep his mind kept playing the humiliation tape, and Matt dreamed of his revenge. Dawn cautiously broke.

Ed came back down the road on his way to work. He noticed a bundle at the end of the Johnsons' driveway. It was oddly out of place. As he approached, the shape took recognition. There appeared to be someone or something in a chair. Ed drove by slowly. It was just too odd. He turned back. He called out. Nothing moved. Nothing stirred. Ed approached. He was sure this was a person. He shook the shoulder—nothing. He pulled back the blanket, now expecting the worst. The blanket slid to the ground. Ed stared. Matt stared back, his eyes frozen in place, his body rigid as ice, the gun cold, cold steel.

Father and Child Reunion

JAKE HAD KILLED men, but he wasn't a bad man. I was checking voicemail and I recognized the number, but I didn't expect the voice. The voice was underwhelmed, hesitant, and cracked with fear. *Wow*, I thought, *the man is exposing himself.*

I met Jake more than twenty years ago. He had just gotten out of prison. He started hanging outside of a Drop-In I was associated with. He would stand in the alley by the back entrance and literally growl at people. His eyes would cut through anyone who dared make contact. His body language challenged anyone to walk within arm's distance. He literally scared the hell out of anyone entering his sphere of gravity. He especially hated authority. Staff needing to tend to their nicotine habit had to endure a hateful scan of their every move. He had everyone looking at their feet and speaking in hushed tones, which only piqued Jake's paranoia, and he'd intimidate the staff. "Who you looking at?" "What did you say?" All done with a snarl and the intimidation of a bite.

Jake was the oldest of ten, the son of a murderer. When his father just up and disappeared, no one cried, but then there was no money. Jake's mother did what many poor, overwhelmed mothers did in the sixties. She gave her son away. She gave him to the state of Minnesota. For no other reason than Jake was born to a no-good man and an anxious, depressed mother, he found himself at the Boys Training School in Red Wing, Minnesota.

The training school was the state institution for wayward boys. Orphans, throwaways, miscreants, and truly bad-asses were all thrown together in one institution and let the strongest survive.

Jake was twelve when the big gates opened and consumed the scared little man. He soon learned that the place was called a school, but it was hell. Beatings and gang rapes commenced. The tearing of his rectum emptied his soul. The beatings permanently injured his hearing and damaged his humanity. He learned that the world spun around violence, and the craziest and meanest won. Jake beat, punched, and kicked his way through adolescence. The other young animals learned to leave Jake alone. He had the reputation of exploding easily, and his victims didn't recover quickly and rarely completely.

Jake endured his purgatory until his eighteenth birthday. He had committed no crime. He was just unwanted. He walked into the institution a scared kid, and he was going to walk out on his birthday a man. He did. The state didn't have the same clear vision. They declared Jake an escapee, and he was run down and chased like a scurvy dog. He was taken back to Red Wing to await a court appearance.

Jake wasn't going to wait. He was impulsive and reactive, behavioral adaptations that had kept him alive. Jake walked to a building on the campus he found completely unnecessary and torched it. Jake found a court date and was shipped to the St. Cloud Reformatory to begin his college education.

Jake humbly but proudly once told me he thought he had killed at least two men in the reformatory. He wasn't sure because he was never charged with anything. On the other hand, the losers were such assholes that even the guards looked the other way when Jake began dismantling them, turning their human forms into pulp.

Psychiatrists said Jake was a psychopath and would never be rehabilitated. Jake aged out of the reformatory and was transferred to Stillwater Prison for his graduate education. At each stop on the road to a prison PhD, Jake became the newbie and the guy who had to establish his reputation to live. He was up to the task. Jake spent most of his big-boy prison years in the hole. He destroyed people to get to the security and sanctuary of solitary. Alone with his thoughts, he began to write poetry—beautiful poetry, filled with passion, love, and human needs for warmth and compassion, subjects he had no real clue about. They were just words, but beautiful words.

Jake entered institutional care a young teen. He exited well into manhood. He entered a scared and scarred kid, and he walked out an animal on the prowl. He was standing at the back door of the Drop-In, challenging anyone to speak, especially anyone who had any kind of authority. He, in fact, hoped a confrontation would happen. Outside prison he had no rep, he had no money, and he was triggered to go off hard on someone.

Over the years, time and marijuana calmed Jake down to where he could tolerate the presence of other human beings. He didn't necessarily like them, but he didn't lash out either. We began talking. He was intrigued with the idea that I was the son of a cop. I found his story and poetry fascinating. We spun around each other like heavyweights waiting to see who would throw the first punch. It became a stalemate, and he begrudgingly allowed me into his orbit. That's how I convinced Jake to take a twenty-six-hour bus ride to freedom.

The fortieth anniversary of the Walk for Poverty in D.C. was going to be marked by a celebration on the Capital Mall. A local agency working with the poor had gotten a grant to take a bus load of people to D.C. Jake asked to go. He had a strange sense of patriotism and wanted to see Washington. He knew the trip would be a challenge. He not only didn't care for most people, but he hated to feel hemmed in. He could not stand to have any too near, especially behind him. Noise, tight quarters, and people moving as herds triggered him. It built a serious agitation that he could not always control. But he needed to see Washington and he was willing to withstand the stress and pressure.

Thirteen hours into the trip, the joy and wonder of the adventure had been melted by the endless chatter of nonsense, the stench of sixty bodies unwashed through the night, and cramps. Butt and leg cramps from the long ride and tight quarters. Brain cramps from the continuous banality of it all. The bus pulled in for a quick toilet and smoke break. I was walking around the blacktop working out my mind cramps when the bus driver approached. "That friend of yours. The big guy with the tattoos, he talking about hurting others. I was standing next to him in the john, and he's muttering about all the f…ing jerks he's going to hurt."

My first reaction was "Where can I get some marijuana?" Then my conscious mind kicked in and reminded me I could lose my professional licensure if I scored some and got it to Jake. Still, it'd be worth it. Dope was the only thing that could keep Jake in a nonviolent mood at times. He had tried prescription meds to kill the anxiety, but he didn't like the feeling. He didn't know calmness and didn't trust it. Marijuana worked so well for Jake that the cops tended to overlook the bags and pipes in Jake's apartment on their frequent visits. They knew that the difference between a cooperative con and a deadly con was green.

I hurried to the restrooms. Jake was coming out. I threw both arms up in an attempt to signal him to stop. I wanted to suggest he seek out some herbal remedy, but before I could speak, he pushed past and turning laughed. "Don't worry, I scored some dope."

We had twenty-four hours in Washington. Jake spent them alone. He wandered among the monuments and said he felt overwhelmed and angered standing at the Wall. The ride home was as bad as the ride out. I found myself at 4 a.m., sitting in the rear of the bus talking to Jake. Now, Jake was very homophobic. Prison does that to men. All the forced and degrading sex gives them a bad taste in their mouths. Literally. Jake knew the rapes had nothing to do with homosexuality, but he had to blame it on something.

Jake began reciting his poetry. I leaned in close as he spoke in hushed tones not to disturb the sleeping. His words were touching and sensitive and belied his armored exterior. He paused for a second. I leaned in closer. "Jake, I know how you feel about gays, but what do you think people are going to say about us? I'm sitting here in a flowered shirt, and you're whispering sweet nothings into my ear." F...!!!!

So in a long and drawn-out way, I've been explaining my concern with the voice I heard on the phone.

"When did I last talk to you? Did I tell you about my heart?"

"Yeah, you did. How you feeling?."

"I had two more stents put in."

"What, when?"

"I was having a checkup and my chest started to hurt."

"Shit."

"Sucks to get old." Then there was a pause. "My kids called me."

Jake hadn't seen his kids since they were toddlers. When I would ask if he wanted to find them, the tough guy would shrug it off. I think he was afraid they'd reject him. Their mother had filled them with venom, and Jake admits he wasn't much of a father. He was pleased they had reached out to him.

Here's Jake's story about his wife. They both drank. When they drank they both became violent. They fought their way through ten years of marriage. Jake almost killed a man over his wife. He laughs now. He suspected she was seeing someone on the side. He knew where the man drank. One night Jake hid under a footbridge the man used to get home from the bars. Jake took a bottle along to get his angry and violent self lubricated for action. He had a butcher's knife, and he was going to slash and castrate the man. He heard him coming and started up the knoll of grassy land, but, drunk, he rolled back down. Too many drinks saved a man's life and kept Jake from going to prison for life.

Jake had settled his family in a small house near

the freeway. Drinking, pissing and moaning, and too often fighting was the evening's activity. In a drunken rage Jake's wife threatened to kill herself rather than continue living with an asshole. Jake beat her down with words and challenged her to act rather than talk. She ran from the house, climbed a fence, and sat down in the lane of oncoming traffic. Jake carries a lot of guilt. The kids grew up with relatives and carry a lot of anger.

Now Jake is at a serious crossroads. His health is deteriorating rapidly. His kids want to know him. They need time to trust him. They want to slowly pick away at the years of anger. Does he have the time?

It's a Wonderful Life

THE WINTER WINDS blew a solitary note of loneliness. Jamie sat at a single-pane window and wondered aloud what Christmas was like in prison. This was the eighth Christmas Eve of her life, and each one had been celebrated without a father. When she would inquire, her mom would hastily and nastily reply, "You're lucky you've never met the SOB. The degenerate belongs in prison."

Jamie blew on the glass and it fogged over. She began an absentminded game of tic-tac-toe. Her stomach rumbled and she held a hand over rolling muscles, quelling the spasm. She hated holidays. School was her sanctuary. On schools days, she ate. If she got to school early enough, there was breakfast and then always lunch. Nights and weekends meant making the most of the sandwiches or desserts she would secret home from school. The present winter break was into its third night. She had eaten her hidden food stocks the first two days. She was hungry.

She turned slowly, hoping to catch a loving glance or a gentle smile from her mother. She was dissociating again. In real life her mother snored, saliva running from the corners of her mouth. She lay across a crumpled chair, her legs splayed and her arms fallen over the chair wings. The "old lady" was lost in a drug stupor, and Jamie wondered how other children experienced Christmas.

Jamie picked up Otis, her stuffed bear. Otis was her comfort and strength. She carried him quietly into the kitchen of their tenement and began one more fruitless search for food. She looked in each cupboard once again. She opened the door of the refrigerator three times, hoping something would magically appear. She looked through the trash and found at the very bottom a piece of bread crust she had missed. She took a small bite and then offered Otis his turn. Otis declined and Jamie devoured the hardened bread.

Jamie walked back to her seat at the window. Snow was falling. Jamie thought about Santa. She had heard about him forever, and she could close her eyes and imagine his large smile and laughing belly. She had never met him. He had always forgotten her home. Christmas in Jamie's house was like any other day. Boredom was the most common experience. Mom had occasional man friends, some of them scary. They always brought drugs or alcohol. Sometimes there were fights, but most of the time, Jamie went to bed and when she awoke, adults were lying in their own

IT'S A WONDERFUL LIFE

vomit on the floor. "Merry Christmas," she said to herself, chasing away the depression of a bleak world.

The apartment had one reminder of the special season. A single holiday card was taped to the refrigerator. It simply said, "Love Ya Babe." It was signed by Bobby, Mom's last week friend. There had been two since him. Jamie had learned early not to trust adults. They weren't dependable.

Jamie's mother began to stir. Her eyes opened. She looked around in disbelief and wiped the spittle from her mouth. She groaned as she shifted. "Come here."

Even though she wasn't focused on Jamie, Jamie went to her. She lifted her butt and reached under the cushions. She handed Jamie a five-dollar bill. "Get me some cough medicine. I'm not feeling good." Jamie hesitated. "Damn you, little brat, move it." Jamie's mom barely got the words out before she fell back in a fog.

Jamie set Otis by the window and admonished him to watch for her return. She pulled a sweatshirt over her head, added a thin coat, pulled her hands up into the sleeves of her vestments, and walked out into the cold. The air was bitter. A light snow was falling. In the streetlights it was pretty, the snow dancing on the wind. She turned into the alley. At the far end was the Gas and Go. Jamie did most of her mother's shopping there. She began to hum to herself a carol. Her shoes had holes in the soles, and already snow was creeping in, melting and setting her toes ablaze with cold. She walked at a brisk pace.

She was almost running, jumping to avoid the darkest shadows. Halfway down the alley way, on the right-hand side, stood two large garbage bins, side by side. Jamie always gave them a wide berth. Sometimes stray dogs would be scavenging around them. Jamie had been frightened by them. Their barks and growls were mean. She didn't need to be bitten to understand their hunger. She shared it. She slowed her pace to a creep. If there were any hungry dogs about, she didn't want to catch their notice. As she approached the bins, she saw two feet sticking out on the far side. She hesitated. Fear overtook the cold. She stopped, weighing her choices. She could run home and avoid whoever was on the other side, or she could run past as fast as she could. She chose to run ahead. If she didn't get her mom's medicine, well, she couldn't think about that. She knew that meant certain pain, and getting past the trash bins was uncertain pain. She sprinted. She felt the wind carrying her. She was faster than Santa's sleigh. Her left foot hit some ice, and her feet went before her. She landed on her back with a thud. It knocked the wind out of her. She whimpered and the feet behind the bin moved.

"You okay?" A dark, heavy voice came from the deepest shadows. Jamie rolled to her knees and slowly began to stand. "That was a heavy fall for such a little one." A man sat forward from the dark. He was old, with a dirty white beard. His head was covered by an old hat, the brim hiding his face. His clothes were well worn and tired. He smelled of whiskey and urine.

"I'm okay," Jamie said and then winced as she put weight onto her left ankle. She pulled her leg up and moved the ankle slowly in circles. It felt better. She took two uncertain steps.

"Where ya going? You're too young to be out on a night like this." He coughed. It sounded like a small spasm. He lit a cigarette. In the light Jamie saw litter surrounding the man as he sat. He must have been dumpster diving. Trash was his throne. He sat on a piece of cardboard. At his knee was a box from KFC. It looked empty.

"I've got to get my mom some medicine." Jamie looked ahead twenty yards to the safety of the store lights.

"Your mom sick?" the man said as he exhaled.

"I'm not supposed to talk to people I don't know." Jamie was defiant.

"You know me. Every kid knows me." Again he coughed.

"I don't know you, I have to go." She started to walk away, hugging the wall on the far side of the alley.

"Hey, kid, look at this." He pulled on his beard. "You really don't know who I am? Hell, I'm out here because of you and your like. Who in their right mind would want to be out on Christmas Eve when they could be home with their family?" It was a statement, but it sounded like a question.

"I can't talk to you. I have to go now." She took another step.

He started to stand, lost his balance, and fell back. "Hey, kid, I'm Santa Claus."

"You're not Santa; there is no Santa." She meant it.

"Well, I'm not *the* Santa. But we all work together. You don't really think one Santa can get to every kid in the world. It takes a team. I'm Ned Claus. Santa's great uncle by marriage. He sent me to this hick town." He burped.

"I don't believe you. There is no Santa. I know! Santa has never given me anything. Santa has never come to my house." She slipped a tear. "He's a fake and a lie."

"What's your name, kid?" He slid back against the wall, exhausted.

"I'm Jamie."

"Jamie what?"

"Jamie Jamison."

"Jamie Jamison. Kid, I've been looking for you for years. You must move a lot. That's why I can't ever find you. You've got to leave an address, kid. Santa ain't a mind reader."

"You're not Santa and I'm not supposed to talk to you."

"Okay then, kid. You get nothing again this year."

"You've never given me nothing. Not last year, not

IT'S A WONDERFUL LIFE

ever. Leave me alone. Santa's not real."

"Like I said, kid, I'm Ned Claus. I've been looking for you for years. You know why I'm sitting here? I was looking over the side of my sled, looking for you, and the deer made a steep climb to the left and I fell out. So, here I am. I fell out of the sky and landed on my butt trying to find you, and all you want to do is argue with me and tell me Santa isn't real. You're hard, kid. You're really hard."

"Yeah? Where is your sled? Where's the reindeer now?"

Ned caught his breath and held it for a bit. Then he felt around on the ground. His hand hit the KFC box, and he held up a drumstick, nothing but bone. He seemed to focus. "See this, kid? This is a magic reindeer bone. Before Rudolph, before any of them, the mightiest deer ever was Midnight Savage. He took Santa through the worst storms for centuries, through the worst snows ever. When he died, Santa gave each of his helpers one of the Savage's bones. All I have to do is blow on this, and all the reindeer in the world will hear it and come running. So all I have to do is blow this and my team will be back and you will never see me again."

"You're lying. That's just an old chicken bone."

"Lying, lying, listen to this."

He put the bone up to his lips and he blew. His face contorted he blew so hard. Then he blew again.

"See, you were lying. I didn't hear anything. You're

just like all those other old people. You all lie."

"Look, little girl, you didn't hear anything 'cause this is a magic reindeer bone. The sound is so high, only reindeer can hear it. They'll be here any minute. Just wait."

"I can't, my mom needs her cough medicine. You're a liar anyways." She ran for the store. As she left the alley she heard him call, "I'll leave you a gift, kid. But I've got to get going. I've got hundreds of stops yet tonight." Jamie ran as fast as she could. She went into the store and got the cough medicine. She handed the clerk the money. He gave her two cents back. She gulped hard. She had hoped to buy some candy. She was so hungry.

She stuffed the package into her pocket and set out into the cold. She entered the alley quietly and stopped to listen. Nothing. She looked hard into the shadows, but it was too dark to see. She walked slowly, putting down one foot and listening and then the next. She flattened herself against the far wall as she came back upon the garbage bins. She hesitated and heard nothing. She whispered. "Hey, mister?" There was nothing. She moved closer. Not a sound. She squeezed her eyes tighter to peer into the dark. He was gone. She felt sad. She had allowed her childish nature to want to believe. He was gone. She had been fooled by a grown-up again. She looked at her feet and felt tears on her cheeks. She swabbed the tears with her sleeve and then she noticed something. An arrow had been drawn in the snow, and it pointed beneath the garbage bin. She found an old curtain rod lying among the clutter, got down on the ground, and poked at something under the bin. She pulled it out. It was an old hanky that had been rolled and tied together. She pulled it apart and found a small locket and chain. The locket was old and scratched. She opened it. Money was crumpled inside. It had been folded a hundred times. She pulled it apart and let out a squeal. She had ten dollars in her hand. Ten dollars! She jumped and danced in the snow and ran the rest of the way home.

She burst into her home, and then she remembered her mother. She looked across the room to Otis, who stood guard at the window. She put a finger to her lips to shush him, then walked on her toes to her mother's chair. She put the medicine at her feet and turned away. She whirled back around, took out the locket, and wrapped it around the bottle of cough syrup.

She ran to Otis and hugged him to her chest. She thought she was going to squeeze the life out of him. She carried him into her bedroom and turned on the TV and lay on her bed. She pulled the covers over to warm up. She put her hand into her pocket and felt the ten-dollar bill. It brought calmness to her mind. Tomorrow she could eat. To still her heart she took a great comforting breath and held it. She felt warm and in control. She looked up at the TV and bounced a little. Her favorite Christmas show was just starting. The old black-and-white film was coming to life, and she clapped as the title rolled across the small screen: *It's a Wonderful Life*.

Red and Purple Hearts

PURPLE HEARTS ARE hard won. The one in Haggerty's Pawn had pulled extra duty for its second Christmas season. Jack, the shop owner, had kept it in his front window, off in a corner near some DVDs and an old pocket watch. It sat there gathering dust and fading with the sun's rays. Each of the past two Christmases, Jack would move it to the center of his display, and it became an eye-catcher. Shoppers who would usually glance in the window and scurry on would stop in their tracks at Christmastime and stare long and hard at the "badge of courage." Half of these shoppers would come into the small store and ask how the Purple Heart ended up in a pawn window. Jack had a handful of stories prepared to entertain them with. Customers seemed moved by his fabricated tales of honor, love, and redemption. Most of the shoppers felt the need to buy some small piece of merchandise to pay Jack back for his time and indulgence. Jack knew that the Purple Heart was his lucky charm. His gross sales at Christmas had increased by nearly 60 percent just because of the curiosity the medal piqued. In fact, sales had been so brisk this day, he thought about shutting down early and stopping at the Legion for a bump or two.

He made a move toward the back room when the bell on his door rang, announcing more money might be coming to his pocket. A young woman entered. The setting sun blurred her image as she moved from the doorway and walked down the crowded aisles. She moved slowly, feigning interest but never really looking at anything. She was nervous. Most people new to a pawnshop come with that stilted gate. They either are carrying their own painful story or they're quite aware that these "poor people's banks" are often last and desperate stops. Dreams end in pawnshops.

As she moved into the shadows of the store, Jack saw she wasn't an unattractive woman. Her face was lean with high cheekbones, and her lips were full. She moved with tension. She fumbled with her mittens and scarf as she stood in front of Jack. Her first words were delicately soft. Jack asked her to speak a little louder as he was an old rock n roller.

She smiled with a small laugh. She spoke again haltingly.

"That Purple Heart. Can I ask how it got here?"

Jack leaned back and decided on a story. "Everyone does." At the last second he switched from the jilted G.I. to the old man story. It rolled off his lips like the truth. Once a story is told, it becomes the listener's truth? Jack had always thought so, and that was why the words flowed so convincingly. He concluded the story with "so I gave the old-timer a few extra dollars so he could go down to the bar and buy his old friends a round." Jack sat back to measure his words' effect.

The young woman was moved by the story; she bit her lips and in her near whisper of a voice said "thank you" and turned. She wiped a tear from the corner of her eye.

"It almost makes me cry too, even though I've shared that tale a dozen times," Jack said. She turned back and politely smiled. She took two steps toward the door and almost as an afterthought she spun slowly around and approached Jack again.

"Do you have any others," she said almost sadly.

"Stories?" asked Jack.

"No… Medals. I'm looking for a particular one. A Purple Heart that would have so much meaning to me. It belonged to my friend."

Jack knew from the sound of her words that this "friend" must have been someone special. Longing had strangled her words as she struggled to force them out.

"Your friend, what can you tell me about him?"

She sighed. "It really doesn't matter." She stared at the cracks in the linoleum floor.

"Well, it is Christmas Eve and I have nowhere to go in particular," Jack half lied as he swept his hand across the space of the room. "This place comes with so many stories; I'd like to hear yours."

"My story, it's really not that interesting."

"Come now," said Jack. "Your story brought you here; it must be worth sharing just this once."

"Well, it's not even a story. I'm looking for a medal that belonged to an old boyfriend. I shouldn't have said old; he was very special. Dave and I dated for two years in college. We looked at each other from across a classroom on the second day of school and we both just knew. It was never said between us, but I knew we were going to be married. We felt so special when we were together. We had dreams."

"And did you…get married?" quizzed Jack.

"No, no, he felt the need to join the service, and after time we lost each other. Somehow life happens, and we just get lost." She began to sniffle.

"Why did you ask about the medal," Jack asked, shifting his weight.

"He came to this town two years ago looking for me. He came to my parents' house on Christmas Day. He gave me some earrings in a small box, and there was a pawn ticket stuck to it. I have forgotten the name of the store… He saw combat and he suffered afterwards. He couldn't keep a job, and our friends think he was homeless. He showed up randomly at others' homes. He was just wandering. He told others he was coming for me…and no one had the heart to tell him I had married. He knocked and I just happened to open the door. He smiled and his eyes were bright as he stood there in his old army coat. He handed me the gift and then my husband came to see who had come, and I introduced him to Dave. Then all the light left Dave's eyes, and he just turned and walked away. I always think of him, especially now at Christmas. I knew he had been wounded. I just thought maybe he had been here. Maybe the earrings were from here. I was curious, that's all."

No more was said in those awkward seconds. She turned quietly and walked to the door. She opened it and the bell rang announcing her departure. Jack called out, "Hey, girlie, come here."

She returned and leaned on the counter supporting her with hope.

"You say he was wounded."

"Yes, more than once I think. He was in Iraq and Afghanistan."

"And you think he was homeless and he had come here, to this town, two years ago."

"Yes," she demurred.

"Well, you know, honey, I think you've come to the right place. Two years ago a hungry young man came to me on Christmas Eve. He was homeless, cold, and desperate. There was a great sadness about him. You could see a yearning in his eyes. He said he was passing through, but then almost as if he were just talking to himself he said, 'I hope I will be staying,' and his eyes came alive with fire."

The young woman leaned closer to Jack. "My friend would have been about thirty; he was six feet and an average build. But he had a scar here." She traced a line down the bridge of her nose.

"That sounds like him," Jack said. "He had on army fatigues. I teased him because they were desert camouflage and he was hoofing it across the Snowbelt. I could tell from his looks he had no money. So I let him stand around and warm himself, and we began bullshitting. He seemed like a nice young man. But he was lost. He mentioned he had come to town to find his one true love. I remember how he cried a tear as he spoke those words. Yes, his one true love." Jack offered a paper towel to the woman to dry her tears. He continued. "He was looking in the case here and spied some pearl earrings. They were pearl, right?"

"Yes, pearl, with antique gold posts."

"Yes, with gold posts, just like those you're wearing."

"Oh, yes," she said, the tears larger and more frequent. "These are the ones!"

"He asked the price, but I knew he didn't have any money. So I lied about the price. I lowered it substantially and then I asked what he had to trade. He offered his backpack and his sleeping bag, but I knew he still needed those. He offered a ring, but it had no value and he knew it. He then reached into his pocket and held out that Purple Heart. I said, 'NO, man, I can't take that.' And he says it doesn't matter because he was wounded three times and he has two more just like this one. And then he said he was really trading an injured heart for the chance to find love again. Man, he had me squalling like a baby. So I took the medal and I gave him those earrings and ten dollars. I was hoping he'd eat."

"But you said that you got that medal from an old man."

"That's because I can't bear to tell this story. It tears at my guts. But it was his medal, and I want to give it to you."

She left smiling and reassured. "Merry Christmas," Jack called to her. He then closed up, took some money from the till, and started out for the Legion. He rubbed his leg as he closed the door. The cold always made those old shrapnel wounds from Nam hurt like a son of a bitch.

Sins of the Father

STAN APPLETON WAS a lonely man. He came to town to bury his grandson. He stood on the steps of the mortuary awaiting his family. As the patriarch he had arrived early to stake his claim as leader and to help the weaker members of his family get through this mess.

Stan looked down State Street and thought it unusually quiet for a Monday morning. When a car would pass, Stan would hang his head in shame and mutter, "Goddamn kid." Stan had gotten a haircut and wore a tie, to look respectable when his grandson was buried. "Goddamn kid."

Stan had been down at the Legion a week ago when his wife, Arliss, called and told him to hurry home. Arliss had been shopping. When she returned home she noticed the message light on her phone was blinking. She picked up the receiver and cautiously pressed the message button. A voice came at her so strong, so needy, it took a moment for her to realize it was Trevor, her only grandson. She froze after hearing the message. She felt her throat tightening and felt nauseous, but she listened again. "Grandma, Grandpa," the voice pleaded, "I'm in big trouble. I need to talk. Please call me right away." Arliss thought Trevor sounded pained. She didn't know how to react, so she called Stan.

Stan paid for his last beer and walked to his car. The only time family seemed to need him was when they wanted money. He resented that none of them could talk to him about their lives or the everyday stuff; he was only sought out when there was trouble.

Stan walked into his middle-class home, with all the trappings of middle-class success. His wife still stood by the phone. He could see the panic in her eyes. But then she was always panicked about something. She handed Stan the phone without explanation and pushed the message button. Stan heard his grandson's plea. He pressed the button a second and then a third time. Turning to Arliss he shrugged his shoulders. "So what?"

Arliss's panic turned to tears. "He sounds scared. Shouldn't we call him? Call him now, Stan. He needs something. What do you think is wrong?" Stan had been married more than thirty years, and it seemed a day did not go by that Arliss didn't have a crisis. He had learned early in their relationship that the quickest way to mollify his wife was to do what she asked and then go off by himself and enjoy some part of the day. Stan called Trevor. No one answered. "No one home," he said to Arliss and threw his hands up.

"Call again. Please call again. I just know something is wrong." Stan did as Stan always did and obeyed. He called the same number, in the same manner, and got the same response. He turned to Arliss with that dog-eared pity in his voice, but before he could speak, the phone rang.

Stan answered with some irritation in his voice. "Hello."

"Hi, is this the Appletons?" The voice sounded very professional.

"Yes, this is Stan Senior."

The voice changed. It came back slower and with a serious tone. "I'm with the Sheriff's Office. I regret to inform you that your son Trevor has killed himself."

"He's not my son."

"What…?"

"He's not my son; he's my grandson. His father is Stan Junior."

"I'm so sorry."

"That's okay; I'll call my son and have him call you."

"Thank you, Mr. Appleton."

"It's quite all right." Stan hung up.

He turned to Arliss. "Get your coat. We're going over to Junior's house. Trevor is dead."

Stan shuffled his feet. Where was that damn mortician? He looked at his watch. There were twenty minutes left before the family was to gather for a private service. The wind picked up and the flag began flapping. Stan made a gun with his hand and pointed his finger at the flag. He shot an imaginary hole, dead center in the stars.

Stan was a war veteran. He didn't talk about it. His closest friends didn't even know he'd served and won some medals. Stan didn't dwell in the past. He was drafted right after high school. When he received his papers to enlist, he was grateful. Arliss had just broken up with him again for the umpteenth time. The town was a dead end. Stan was relieved. He didn't have to make excuses or try to explain his need to leave. The Army had taken him out of his boredom.

Stan found he actually enjoyed the structure and regimen of the Army. He thrived in the controlled chaos. When others shuddered at the sergeants' rants, Stan secretly smiled. No sergeant was as tough as his old man. Stan became a squad leader and was shipped off to Nam. He got hooked on the adrenaline of combat and re-upped twice more.

Stan knew he was an action junkie. He liked taking point. When the "shit" came down, he always was out front. No job was too dangerous. He volunteered for it all. Other soldiers were in awe of his courage, but they also understood Stan was crazy.

Stan returned home from three tours. He burned

his uniform, put his medals out of sight, and drank a few beers more than he needed to. About a month after his homecoming, he ran into Arliss again. She was working as a secretary at the school. Stan took a job at the printing plant, and he and Arliss married.

Stan was numb to emotions, so he never was quite sure if he loved Arliss, but she was convenient. They settled into the routine of married life and eventually started a family.

Stan hadn't had a cigarette in more than six months. If the rest of the damn family didn't get to the mortuary in the next ten minutes, Stan swore to himself he would start smoking again. He was agitated with the whole bunch. He seemed to always be agitated about something, but usually it was family. They always managed to disappoint him. He found some gum in his pocket, so he unwrapped it. He put the gum in his mouth and threw the paper to the ground. The wind rolled the wrapping out into the street and blew it toward the center of town.

Stan watched the paper bounce along. Just like his life. He was never headed in any particular direction; he just rolled with the times. He remembered once telling Arliss he loved her. It was on their wedding night in the middle of their great passion. She had seemed as anxious as he was to get it over with. When the act was completed, he wanted to say thank you but felt that was trite. So he shared an "I love you." It would be the only time he would be so expressive.

He checked his watch. Arliss was late. That was her M.O., so Stan didn't get angry. She was always late. He laughed a little inside and wished she had married someone else, or that she had been late enough to the wedding that he could have left the altar in righteous indignation.

Stan and Arliss would have a "good" relationship. There just wouldn't be a lot of joy. Stan didn't like intimacy. It scared him. He wasn't conscious of it. He just felt his chest tighten and palms get sweaty whenever an emotion was expressed. Intimacy made him feel vulnerable. Sometimes when he let his guard down, memories and dreams of Nam intruded into his life and scared him, so it was better to keep everyone at a distance.

Arliss drove into the parking lot. She waved and Stan nodded. He could see her gathering her purse and things. He walked toward her and politely asked if he could help her with anything. She politely responded, "No." The door to the mortuary opened, and the director stuck his head out and offered a warm greeting. Stan suggested that Arliss go in and he would keep watch for the others. Arliss squeezed Stan's hand and he squeezed hers back. She was being a trooper. She could be strong.

Stan continued his watch. He hoped that Junior and his wife, Sarah, would be the next car to come along. When it wasn't he leaned back against the building. He rubbed his hands and smiled that they had just touched Arliss's.

Stan knew Arliss loved him. He didn't know how deeply. He also was faintly aware that she was always angry, and he suspected it was because of him.

Over the years Arliss had developed a deep appreciation for Stan and felt committed to the relationship. She couldn't imagine herself in any other circumstances. She also could not acknowledge her anger toward him. She tried when they had first married to change him. She wanted to be close. She wanted to be able to share her thoughts and feelings. When she realized that Stan could never become intimate, she became angry. She felt he had abandoned their relationship and she knew in her heart that he had betrayed the love they could have had.

Arliss had worked very hard to reach Stan. But Stan was never available. When Arliss was most frustrated or needed Stan's strength and understanding, he would become more distant. Everything in their relationship had been compromised. Stan grew more distant, and Arliss developed a chronic anger. Unable to express the anger, Arliss chose to be treated for depression.

Stan had night terrors from the beginning of their married life. Prior to their first anniversary, they had gotten separate beds so that Arliss could sleep. She at first had tried talking to Stan about his dreams, but he refused to share.

When Arliss would become extremely angry at Stan for his unavailability, she would remember the great pain in him, and she would become very protective of him. Quickly their marriage had become an association of caretakers, both worrying about not upsetting the other, and hiding any feelings that would disturb the peace of their coexistence.

A motorcycle approached and caught Stan's attention. He had always wanted a bike, but he also knew he would have killed himself had he owned one. He could be impulsive, and that coupled with his anger would have led to an early demise, so now he just admired bikes from a distance.

In their third year of marriage, Stan Jr. was born. A year later Page completed the family. Each child brought occasional joy to his life, but he feared truly attaching because everyone eventually disappointed Stan. He just knew his kids would be no different.

Stan did know the expectations of being a good parent. He encouraged the kids' participation in sports and community groups. He attended everything they had ever been a part of. He yelled and cheered for them. In public he was very supportive as he knew that was expected. At home he continued to struggle with intimacy. The dinners were usually quiet affairs.

When Junior was five or six, he had found Stan's medals and asked a hundred questions. Stan did not give one answer. Junior noticed Stan's uneasiness about the war and Stan's participation. These things became taboo in the family. Children were to be seen and not heard, especially not allowed to ask sensitive questions.

As Junior aged, he became disquieted by the unspoken and he felt distant and unloved by his stoic father. As a teen he began to rebel and had several scrapes with authority. When Stan felt disappointment, and when those feelings were caused by Junior, Stan could go into a rage. Stan had often raised his hand to Junior, and he excused his behavior as Junior needed to learn to be respectful. Arliss had been aware of the rages in Stan, but she knew better than to question them. She shuddered when her son was injured by her husband, but to name the rage was to ask for pain. So Stan's anger and sometimes violence became taboo.

Page was a bright and cheerful child. She always attempted to get close to her father. She made it her life's goal to make him happy. She chose to ignore the coolness of her parents' relationship and created fantasies of better times. When Page began dating, her mother questioned Page's choice in men. When Arliss was sharing her disappointment and concerns, Page became protective and would attack her mother with a rage she did not understand.

In quieter moments, Page questioned the value of male relationships. With her father as a role model, she believed all men had a propensity for coolness and rage. She had watched the non-dance of intimacy in her parents' relationship and she felt confusion and distress about sexuality.

Stan spit out his gum and stretched his arms out

from his side. He looked down the street as he twisted and saw Junior approaching with his wife, Sharon, and their daughter, Michelle. Stan gave a little wave. The women waved back. Stan shook the ladies' hands. He started to lean into a hug with his son, but caught himself. They shared politeness and then Junior ushered his family into the mortuary. It all happened too quickly for Stan to say he was waiting for Page's family.

Stan allowed a moment of solace for himself. By all external measures his family was doing well. They all had nice homes. Junior and Page had college degrees, and Junior had followed his dad into the Army.

Stan kicked himself for not saying more to acknowledge Junior. Stan had some anger and resentment yet from Junior's rough adolescent years and had kept Junior at a respectable distance. He didn't want to get to close.

What Stan had missed was that Junior just needed some time and attention. He had longed to be closer to his dad. Junior grew up thinking that men never show tenderness and sometimes need to use a little roughness to keep things respectful. Stan had been Junior's role model. Junior wanted to be just like his dad. Junior, like his father, never showed feelings of fear, vulnerability, or intimacy. He learned early in his life to fear his own anger. He had gotten into a fight in middle school and had seriously injured another child. He vowed to control his anger, and he taught himself to be compliant and passive, especially with authority figures. Trying to impress his father, he had gone to college to join the ROTC.

During Junior's senior year the first Gulf War broke out. Junior felt compelled to join the regular Army. He didn't want to miss the "big show." His family had always been warriors, and he wasn't going to break the tradition.

Junior had called his father, expecting, hoping that his father would be overwhelmed with pride. Stan was overwhelmed with emotion, but Junior could not read it. Arliss had been on the extension, and she was greatly disturbed. She feared losing her only son and she was drowning in her tears, secretly wishing for Stan to man up and tell their son he did not have to put his life at risk. She wanted to scream like a siren so that Stan did not mistake her needs, but she just sobbed and held back saying anything that would betray her husband's life. Stan pulled himself together and told Junior to do his best and "stay safe." Junior hung up. He felt some confusion, but he believed his parents supported him and that he had their blessings.

Junior's only prior experience with war was watching old movies with his father. He remembered his father insisting they watch the movies together, to get some "family time." His father would watch in silence, but Junior could read his reactions to the gooks, and he secretly took on his father's fury for the enemy. Gooks or towel heads. They were all the same.

Junior didn't need the Army's lessons in how to

dissociate fear, vulnerability, and sorrow. He had absorbed those lessons from his father. Junior found safety, security, and love in his brother warriors' arms. In the depths of the war, Junior felt especially close to his sergeant, who reminded him of his father. He knew he would follow this man anywhere. After every firefight Junior would seek the Sarge out, and he developed a closeness he never had with his father.

On a routine patrol, the unit came under fire. Sarge led an assault against entrenched troops shooting from rooftops in a small village. Sarge went down in front of Junior. Junior saw red. A blind rage took control of him, and in the fury of his great loss and grief, he killed all towel heads, including women and children.

Back at the base he began to have feelings of guilt and shame. His comrades in arms covered him with accolades and showered him with stories of his bravery and savageness. He used their love to cover his shame and to bury the incident deep in his psyche. With the incident buried, he poured dirt over the "whys" of his violence, and alongside the "whys," he buried his father's need for vengeance.

Junior stuck his head out. "Dad, you coming in?"

"I'll be along. I'm waiting for Page." Stan looked at his feet. "You and your family spend some time alone with Trevor. I'll be in."

Stan was getting anxious. He had always had an ambivalent relationship with Page. He knew she was currently struggling in her marriage. Arliss had shared that. He wasn't sure how he was to respond to Page when she finally arrived.

Page had reluctantly dated in college. She had met a man who seemed familiar. They dated and he pushed her for sex. Page consented only because it was expected. She became pregnant. She married Earl because it was also expected. A week after their wedding ceremony, Page realized she'd made a big mistake. Earl was even more distant and unavailable than her father. She wanted to run, but then Earl was in need of her protection.

Earl was a good provider, or so Stan had heard. He wasn't much of a conversationalist, so Stan knew practically nothing about Earl. Stan had overheard a whispered conversation between Page and Arliss in which Page confided that her sex life was unfulfilling and that Earl was distant. Stan understood and even smiled. Why should anyone enjoy what he couldn't?

Stan smiled at his little secret and then concealed it as he saw Page approaching. She came alone. Her husband "had to work," and her daughter "had too much schoolwork." Stan knew Page couldn't stand Earl. He also understood that Page's teen daughter Carol had cut herself again. She was currently hospitalized.

"Page." He reached out to hug her. Page stepped back and offered her hand. Stan couldn't help himself. "Where's Carol?" Page cut her father in half with her glare and walked past him into the funeral home.

Stan felt like an idiot. What the hell went wrong? He knew his grandkids were bright, creative souls. They were curious and intelligent. He couldn't understand what went so wrong. He secretly blamed his children, while the children cursed the schools and the communities and their children's friends. No one was going to be too insightful. Getting too close to the truth was to burn with the truth.

Stan knew all the arguments and blame games. He understood that the grandchildren were sensitive, much more sensitive than he or his children. They asked questions and they didn't allow the family secrets to ferment. Stan did blame the schools for that. The grandchildren openly spoke of family taboos and had tried to drag the family into the mud with therapy and medications. The adults resisted the therapy. Family problems were no one's business, not even between family members. Secrets should remain secrets.

Stan could feel some anger building, so he shut it off. He turned to go inside and say goodbye to his grandson. A tear began to form. Stan stopped in his tracks, took a deep breath, and scolded himself. "Don't you fall apart. Your family needs you. Be the rock."

An American Christmas

DALE HAD SPENT his life chasing thunder. He would say to anyone and no one in particular that he had lived his life on the 20/20/20 plan. With a chuckle to himself he'd add, "Twenty years insane, twenty years in prison, and twenty year minding my own business." He stepped outside of Nick's Bar and turned his collar up. The cold took a bite out of his neck and sent a shiver down to his feet. He was two weeks out of rehab and two minutes away from his last drink. He stood at the intersection and watched the wind blow snow devils down the quiet streets. He was unsure of his next steps. A quick pivot and he could continue his life as the devil's son. He kicked a blackened ice block that had fallen from a car. It didn't move and he cursed the pain in his toes. He'd promised the major at the Army he'd help out with the Christmas party. He resented having to keep his word. Stomping his sore foot to get the circulation moving, he noticed a steady stream of individuals walking into the Salvation hall across the street. They were in a hurry. Maybe they were cold or maybe they were hungry. Dale knew he didn't really care to know. Some of them were dragging kids in tow. He had no patience for petulant youths. In fact he was pretty sure he hated most kids.

Foolish or wise, he wasn't sure, but he was hungry, so he followed the herd. He stepped inside the hall and several dozen people milled about, souls lost at the gates of purgatory. An ankle biter with snot running from its nose walked near with a sticky candy cane in one hand. Dale stepped back and let the little vase of fermenting germs pass. He felt his muscles tighten and his jaw clench. Too many people, too much noise, set him on edge.

He stood frozen with his back to the wall. An old woman with the appearance of a Gypsy entered with one ginger child in her arms. She swore like a sailor. They came close but he refused to acknowledge her. Dale kept quiet, fearing they could smell murder on his breath. Anger started to well up and shout in his brain. He stuffed it and moved to the farthest corner, well away from the Christmas tree, where the children were gathering like flies on a carcass. He slid down onto his haunches and looked for the major. He briefly thought it was a good enough reason not to drink if he was going to be making foolish promises while drunk. He glared at the poor patrons and slipped his hand into his coat pocket. The bottle of Wild Turkey comforted his mind and silenced the voices in his head. The voices were like shadows on a cloudy day. He was the Hurricane Boy and the voices were great winds temporarily quieted. He stood in the eye of a gathering storm.

The major approached Dale and handed him a bag with the red suit in it. It smelled like a prison cell, old sweat and piss. The major thanked Dale and whispered instructions into his ear. Dale didn't flinch. He watched the hall fill and the crowd turn into waves of nauseating, malicious ill feeling.

The mass of poverty moved toward the kitchen's serving window, and the major quieted them, except for a squalling baby, and led them in a prayer of thanks. Dale thought, *Nothing is free; everything has a price. Even paradise has its hunters.*

The people received plates of Christmas traditions and moved to the tables. They ate quietly with their heads bowed while a small choir sang the sanguine songs of empty promises and childish dreams. Dale stood and moved quietly to the men's room. He checked for others and then took a slug of the Wild Turkey. The building rage subsided a notch. He put on the red suit and felt the snugness of the red jacket against his beer belly. He completed the disguise with the beard and wig, then sat down on the porcelain stool and waited for his entry cue.

Twenty minutes passed and the opening bars of "Santa Claus Is Coming to Town" drew Dale out of a stupor. He adjusted the wide black belt and stepped

AN AMERICAN CHRISTMAS

out into the dingy gala of a Christmas celebration. Walking through the crowd with little ones giggling and grabbing, Dale didn't know who to swat, the sniveling little ingrates or the irresponsible adult dullards who had born such poor excuses of humanity into this swirling bowl of poverty.

He settled into a large chair set by the decorated tree and watched as awkward parents formed a line with their frightened, expectant children. The first child set on his knee came with a full load in its pants, and Dale fought the urge to spew his stomach contents. The red suit was a siren calling all the little scoundrels to dream. Each child asked for impossibilities, and Dale promised them even more.

The line had reached its end. Dale sat back and drew a tired breath. He looked up as she approached. She flowed through the tables like a water snake. She was small but not a child. Her pale skin hid her age. Her eyes reflected generations of pain. She stood before Dale swaying like a fragile grass in the wind. He held out a hand to steady her, and she fell into his lap. He put his hand on her back, and she straightened like a marionette. With great exhaustion she raised one finger and lightly touched his beard.

"You're not real." The words rang hollow.

Dale shifted, balancing her weight. "What did you expect?"

She looked Dale directly in the eyes, and Dale noticed the accent of death. "I want to be a child."

Unsure of what she had said, Dale gruffly whispered, "What the hell was that?"

She fell forward into his beard. "I want to be a child again. I want another chance. I don't want to live this life anymore." She reached up and stroked the fur brim of his hat. Dale saw the trail of needle tracks up and down her arm. Dale recognized this trial of tears. He moved his hand from her back to her shoulder. He pulled her in and held her for a brief moment. A small cry echoed from her heart, and she slid into a puddle at his feet. He helped her to stand. Dazed she moved back through the tables. Dale felt something. He wasn't sure if it was empathy, but he understood her pain.

Dale sat down again on the porcelain stool and waited for the noise of the crowd to disperse. When it was quiet he walked out. The major was wiping off chairs. He moved to meet Dale and thanked him. Dale avoided taking his hand and hurried outside. The bitter cold burned his cheeks. Dale lit a cigarette and felt some of his tension lessen. On his second drag he heard a stirring behind the large garbage bin. He moved around it. She lay as a babe in a manger, a needle stuck in her arm. Her unconscious stirrings had marked the ground with a snow angel. The moonlight framed her face, and Dale saw the innocence of a time past. He gathered her into his arms. He saw life in her eyes. He smiled. "C'mon, child," and he carried her back into the warmth of the hall.

Copasetic

GERAHTY WAS DEATHLY tired. He was a man who sleep had defriended. He found a parking spot under a street lamp and limped toward O'Hurlys, a neighborhood bar that the neighborhood had deserted with white flight. It was now populated by the homeless, the wounded, and the night stalkers. Gerahty's kind of people.

He stood for a second at the door and breathed in the stale remnants of past cigarettes. He hadn't smoked for a year, but reminders of the burning leaf sent a calmness through his shoulders. He opened the door. Mac, one of the owners, looked up from rinsing glasses. "Hey, Copper, how are you?"

"Copasetic, Mac, copasetic." Gerahty placed his large frame on his stool. He took a quick glance around. All the regulars were pasted firmly in their places. When his world outside was constant chaos, Gerahty found calmness and safety in the consistency of the world inside O'Hurlys.

Mac threw Gerahty a look, and Gerahty tapped the bar with his index finger and quickly flashed Mac two fingers upright. Mac grabbed the Jameson and poured two shots into a highball glass and dropped in exactly one ice cube. Gerahty swirled the drink in the glass, and in one reflexive move, it was gone.

Gladys, the Crab Lady, sat two stools away to Gerahty's left. She let him finish his first drink, then slid her butt off her stool and moved next to Gerahty. Gerahty nodded, smiled, and recalled the first time the Crab Lady invaded his personal space.

Gladys gained her moniker because of her particular deformity. Gladys was born with only two digits on each hand. Her thumb and index fingers were extremely elongated and thick, giving the appearance of pincers. Gladys also had had a split lip and cleft palate. Her lip had been haphazardly sewn together and her cleft left untouched. Her speech sounded as if it reverberated from a deserted corn bin. It clanged and rang about her mouth before coming out as a mismatch of broken English and gibberish. Gladys loved to talk and her words flowed from her mouth as easily as the spit that always drooled from the corners of her lips. Understanding her was another thing.

Gerahty signaled Mac for two. He smiled at Gladys and straightened his stiff back and pulled on the knot in his tie. Gladys reached over with her claw and completed pulling the knot out. Gerahty laughed. "Thanks, Gladys."

Gladys had a high-pitched voice that squeaked like a porpoise trying to quote Socrates. "How was your day?"

"Copasetic, Gladys, copasetic." He ordered another round. Mac slid the drinks down the bar, and Gladys blocked them with her pincer. They clinked their glasses and Gerahty tossed his. Gladys set to nursing hers.

Gerahty leaned in to hear Gladys. Her lips had been moving, but Gerahty hadn't heard anything. He was bent over looking directly at Gladys' lips. He understood a few of the words, "help," "devas," and maybe "Noona." Gerahty looked at Gladys and said, "Noona." Gladys smiled and waved a claw over her head in the direction of a woman sitting in the darkest corner of the bar.

Noona was looking into the bottom of a beer mug. She was lost somewhere in the stale beer. Stuck in the past, frozen from moving forward, she had become a regular. Her shoulders relaxed and she moved over to the jukebox. She fed the machine and began punching buttons. A slow, hypnotic tune began. Noona, dressed in the camouflaged hunting gear of someone much bigger than herself, began to sway. Her feet moved and she slowly whirled around the dance floor, like the seed of a dandelion caught on a summer breeze.

It was difficult to guess her age. Her hair was long, full, and unkempt. She stuffed it under the brim of a hunter's cap. She was slight of build. That's all the clothing allowed anyone to guess. She was a pile of clothes moving in time to the music, unaware of others. She fit the pattern of all the other regulars, unwanted, unknown, just lost souls doing time in this life, sometimes hoping for another chance on another plane, but all secretly fearing this was as good as it would ever get.

Gerahty moved to the dance floor and stood behind Noona as she swayed lost in the peace of the moment. Gerahty didn't want to disturb her tranquility, so he just stood and watched, mesmerized by her hands as they moved slowly, gracefully, spelling out the mystery of thoughts gone, thoughts coming, and thoughts turning around on themselves. He was haunted and enchanted. She bent and rolled like tall grass in a gentle wind. Gerahty stood, a little embarrassed. Noona spun around, facing him, her head down. She lifted her eyes and nodded at Gerahty. "Hey, Copper."

Gerahty shook his head to the left toward a table. Seated, Noona reached for her beer, and Gerahty noticed the scars that crisscrossed her arm and wrist. He'd seen them before, but they always caught him a little off guard. As Noona drank, Gerahty surveyed her face, hidden by her hat and long hair. She wore bangs and her hair fell long against the side of her face, obscuring any view of a profile. It hid her well. Gerahty wasn't sure how old she was. He had known her for many years. He imagined she had been very pretty, and maybe still was, cleaned up.

Whatever this was, Gerahty wanted to keep it simple and short. He was too tired to provide any empathy. He settled his large frame into the chair and leaned into Noona. She drank slowly and emptied her glass. Her speech was slightly slurred. Her eyes seemed locked on some faraway object, but Gerahty knew that wasn't from the drink. "Hey, Copper, how are you, man?"

"Copasetic, Noona, copasetic. I love to watch you dance."

She looked down, embarrassed. Gerahty caught Mac's attention and waved his index in a circle and signaled two. Max got busy.

Noona weaved in her seat and tilted toward Gerahty. "Copper, I think I'm being followed." She suddenly became silent as if she lost her thought. Gerahty waited an awkward second.

"Noona, who's following you?"

"It's nothing, Copper, it's nothing. How you been?"

"Noona, you wouldn't have told Gladys you were scared if this wasn't important. What's going on?"

Noona straightened in her chair. She did not meet Gerahty's eyes. "I think I have a stalker and it's getting a little unnerving. He's a creep."

"Who's a creep?"

"You know that guy that sometimes comes in here wearing the Green Bay hat and has the lazy eye? I think he's called Slanty?" Gerahty nodded. "He's not in here every night, but almost every night I'll see him out on the street. I feel like he follows me. Last night I thought I heard a dog bark and I looked out my window. It was four goddamn a.m. and I saw him. I think it was him, hanging back in the shadows staring right at me."

"How long has this been going on, Noona?" Gerahty sat back as Mac placed drinks on the table.

"The Big Guy paid for the drinks," Mac said as he nodded his head toward The Big Guy sitting at the bar. Noona waved a thanks, Gerahty tipped his glass in a toast, and threw the drink down. The Big Guy smiled.

Gerahty returned his attention to Noona. "What do you want me to do about it, Noona."

"About what?" Noona seemed confused.

"About your stalker."

"I don't know, Copper. You got any advice? It scares me a little."

"Do you want me to talk to him, Noona?"

"Would it do any good?"

"Hell if I know, but maybe if he knows that others know what he's doing, he'll knock it off."

"You know I've got a daughter and I worry about her too. What if it's her that this creep is after?"

Gerahty sat back. "I'll take care of it, Noona. It doesn't matter who he's interested in; he's scaring the hell out you. That alone needs to stop." Noona seemed to go away. Her eyes glassed over and she just stared at the grain in the table.

Gerahty had always been puzzled by Noona. He

knew her history. Her mother had been crippled in an accident when Noona was six. Noona's father turned to Noona for sexual fulfillment. He told Noona she was pretty. Noona felt dirty. Then there was a whole string of rapes. Noona seemed to be a walking target for all the sick perps in the city.

What confused Gerahty was her dance. He couldn't help but feel stirrings when he watched her. He could tell by the look in other men's eyes they felt the same. Noona's dancing was entrancing and inviting. How inviting? Then there were times she'd bring her ten-year-old daughter into the bar. The bar felt like Gerahty's home, but he knew this den of transgressions was no place for a child, particularly a female child. Noona had her history and then she'd bring her daughter into the bar, and the kid would be wearing short shorts and halter tops. What the hell was Noona thinking? Gerahty always felt a private stirring whenever he thought about Noona. He was feeling the warm flush of desire, so he shut off his thoughts and left Noona sitting. "Don't worry about it, Noona, I'll take care of it."

Gerahty stood and steadied himself. He walked up to the bar in short and deliberate steps. He sat on a stool next to The Big Guy. The Big Guy and Gerahty had history. They had been childhood friends and it was The Big Guy who initially brought Gerahty to O'Hurlys.

The Big Guy had developed some kind of brain

or neurological problem early in life. Gerahty never asked what it was, and The Big Guy never felt compelled to share. The Big Guy had slowly deteriorated until he had lost his speech and become stiff and slow in movement. He seemed better early in the day, but as the evenings at O'Hurlys faded into dawn, The Big Guy would become frozen. Gerahty felt it was his duty to get The Big Guy home each night.

As soon as Gerahty was comfortable, The Big Guy slid him a note written on a bar napkin. Gerahty glanced at it while ordering a couple of beers. He said out of the side of his mouth, "I'm fine."

The Big Guy scribbled furiously and slid a new napkin to Gerahty. "Quit shittin me. How are you?"

Mac set the beers down. Gerahty sensed he was trapped by his friend's concern, so he unloaded.

"I'm not sleeping again. Goddamn dreams." He looked at The Big Guy, who looked back, expressionless. "I've seen too damn much. I try to sleep and I hear the screams and I see the faces. It's the girls that get me. There was that young woman who got sliced up by her boyfriend up on the south side. I got to the apartment and he was still chasing her around the place. She was covered in blood and he wouldn't stop. I shot him and he went down hard. I held her and she kept asking if she'd be all right and I kept promising her the ambulance would be there and she'd be fine. She bled out in my arms. Then there was that Puerto Rican girl whose boyfriend set her on fire. I had her wrapped in my coat, and she held on to me as if her life depended on it. She wouldn't let go. When they put her in the ambulance, she pulled me along, so I rode with her to the hospital." He paused, sipped his beer, lowered his voice, and continued, "She didn't make it."

The Big Guy put his hand on Gerahty's shoulder. "They won't leave me alone. If I fall asleep they start screaming. Man, I don't think I've had more than a couple of hours of sleep a night for months. It sucks, man, it sucks." Gerahty almost allowed a tear of self-pity. He sat back and looked at The Big Guy, and The Big Guy was stone. Gerahty placed his hand on The Big Guy's shoulder, and they communicated through the silence.

Noona was dancing again, and Gerahty knew that The Big Guy enjoyed watching as much as he did, so he spun The Big Guy around and they both sat, eyes transfixed on the dance floor.

Gerahty had lost track of time and space. He gradually became aware of someone standing in front of The Big Guy cursing. This guy was loud and aggressive. He had a hand inside his jacket and he was spitting as he shouted at The Big Guy.

"What are you staring at, asshole? Talk to me, you retard. What are you staring at? You'd better say something, mother****er, or you're dead."

Gerahty recognized Slanty. He thought, *Who's the retard? Can't this dirtbag see that The Big Guy can't respond to his bullshit?* Gerahty looked at the hand inside Slanty's coat. He was threatening and he quite possibly had a gun. Gerahty searched his mind for the appropriate response. He looked at the bottle in his hand and watched it arch and land squarely against Slanty's forehead. Gerahty was slightly amused when he looked at Slanty on the floor, blood gushing from a large cut.

Mac and another customer scooped up the bloody man and threw him into the alley. The action had frozen Noona. The rest of the bar patrons hardly noticed. A new song came on and Noona went limp for a second and then fell back into the sexualized trance of her dance.

Gerahty faced The Big Guy. He thought the stone man had a smirk. Gerahty helped his friend to his feet and hailed a cab. He helped The Big Guy get in, paid the fare, and sent his pal home.

He returned to the bar. Gladys waved to him as he walked in the door and signaled another round. Gerahty politely shook his head "no." He stumbled toward a back booth and laid his tired body down. Exhaustion overcame him. Gladys took off her coat and covered him. Noona unplugged the jukebox and sat silently next to Gladys. Mac shushed everyone with a finger to his mouth and a nod in Gerahty's direction. They knew he would only sleep a couple of hours and they also understood he needed it badly. They all smiled at each other. Everything was copasetic.

When Life Gives You Lemons

BILLIE STEPPED OFF his bike, his heel caught the saddle seat, and he fell to the ground. He lay there for a moment allowing the sweat to run down his face. The droplets followed the curve of his lips and seeped into his mouth. He enjoyed the salty brine and rolled over and got on his feet. It was his thirtieth birthday, and he'd taken the day off to just enjoy himself.

Picking up his bike, he turned toward the street as a FedEx truck approached. The driver jumped, hurriedly scanning a long box, and running at a fast walk, he handed the box to Billie and was off again. Billie stared at the box. It was about four feet long and only about eight inches wide. It had his name on it. A return address indicated it came from his father, the Old Man. He hadn't spoken to his father in twenty years.

Billie was one of three children adopted by Jack and Emily Smart. Jack was a professional. He had an air of superiority which he was always cultivating. He was cold and distant with his own children, and to strangers he was just damned arrogant.

Billie set the package aside and showered. The package unsettled him. He was curious but he couldn't shake the feeling that it was an omen. "Why now?" He stepped out of the shower and grabbed a towel that had been hanging on the shower curtain rod. He felt a twinge. "Max," he mumbled.

He hadn't thought about Max for several months. He felt a tear forming, so he caught his breath and cleared his throat. "No more," he said.

Max was Billie's older brother by eight years. Max had a smile that endeared him to everyone, and Billie remembered as a child wanting to be just like his big brother. He had practiced walking and talking like Max. Max was smart and funny. He could take the Old Man's words and twist them in a way that the Old Man would stammer and lose his mind. The Old Man had never hit anyone, but his words destroyed souls and burnt holes in hearts. Max could take it. He would stand toe to toe and spit vindictives back at the Old Man, rat-a-tat-tat. They were like two cobras spitting venom. Max seemed immune to the Old Man's poison. Everyone else withered.

When Max was eighteen he flipped the Old Man off and left the house for good. The Old Man couldn't stand it. His narcissism demanded complete adulation from the family. He started a campaign of phone calls and letters pleading with the prodigal son to return. Bible quotes meant to guilt and belittle became a weapon. Max resisted.

Mom loved all her children. She had convinced Max to try family counseling. The family had endured six sessions of belittling and blaming of Max for all the family's ills by the Old Man. Billie hated the therapist for his inability to put the Old Man in his place and hold him accountable for just being the asshole he was.

The last session any of them attended, the therapist had seemed to grow a pair. He looked the Old Man in the eye after one of his rants about God, heaven, and Max and said calmly but firmly, "Max can't always be the problem." Max broke a smile and the rest of the family tensed as the Old Man leaned forward. He sucked in a big breath. He rolled his eyes as if he were examining his insides and leaned forward with an air of great authority. He started quietly. "You're right, Max isn't the only problem." Was this a moment of clarity, self-confession? The family anticipated supporting Max, finding some wholeness and completeness as a family. Healing words had to flow. "Yes, you're right," the Old Man continued. His right hand came up. His index finger extended. Like a wand of truth he pointed at all in the circle. "You're a problem. You're a problem, and you're a problem." He stood and walked out.

Billie never saw Max again. Billie left home as

soon as he could. He thought of Max but their paths never crossed. He received an envelope one day from the Old Man. It contained an obituary. At age thirty Max had killed himself. The drugs he had been using to cover his pain had failed. Max had taken a gun and ended his life.

Billie dressed. He wandered around his apartment aimlessly. He had some juice and checked his email. His anxiety pushed him to open the package. He did so slowly, cautiously. He folded the paper and set it aside. He opened the box and pulled the gift out and set the box aside. There was a small card. It simply said, "Happy 30th. Dad."

Billie looked down on the gun that had ended Max's life.